REVOLVE: IS THE CYCLE OF LIFE
CONSTANTLY REVOLVING YET
GETTING BOLDER AND BRAVER
WITH EVERY REVOLUTION.
TAKING ON EXPERIENCE WITH
EVERY MOVEMENT. THE FEAR
OF REVERSING ITS PATTERN
AND GOING BACK INSTEAD
OF DISCOVERING THE PAST
WITH ITS FUTURE.

Publishing Director: *Sarah Lavelle*
Editor: *Romilly Morgan*
Creative Director: *Helen Lewis*
Design: *Dave Brown, apeinc.co.uk*
Cover Design: *John Newman*
Design Assistant: *Gemma Hayden*
Picture Researcher: *Katie Horwich*
Production: *Vincent Smith, Tom Moore*

First published in 2015 by
Quadrille Publishing
www.quadrille.co.uk

Quadrille is an imprint of Hardie Grant
www.hardiegrant.com.au

Text © 2015 John Newman
Design and layout © 2015
Quadrille Publishing Limited

The rights of the author have
been asserted.

Cataloguing in Publication Data:
a catalogue record for this book
is available from the British Library.

ISBN 978 184949 650 6

Printed in China

REVOLVE, the album was released globally on October 16, 2015.
Available on CD, download & vinyl

CONTENTS

PART ONE

I HAD A REALLY SPECIAL MOMENT THE OTHER DAY, ONE OF THOSE EXPERIENCES I'LL NEVER FORGET. I WAS BACK IN THE UK AFTER A STINT IN LA, STAYING AT MY HOUSE IN NORTH LONDON. I HAD THE DAY OFF FOR THE FIRST TIME IN AGES AND I JUMPED AT THE OPPORTUNITY TO GET MY STUFF OUT MY FLAT AND SACK OFF MY OVERLY ECCENTRIC AND HIGHLY IRRITATING LANDLORD. I DECIDED TO MAKE A TRIP TO THE CHARITY SHOP WITH LOADS OF OLD CLOTHES I HAD NEVER TAKEN OUT OF CARDBOARD BOXES SINCE I HAD MOVED IN. I CHOSE A CHARITY SHOP THAT I USED TO VISIT A LOT WHEN I WORKED IN THE PUB OPPOSITE, THE OLD DAIRY; IT WAS THE SHOP I USED TO GET MY SUITS FROM WHEN I WAS TOO SKINT TO FORK OUT FOR HIGH STREET CLOTHES, EITHER FOR MYSELF OR MY BAND.

SO, I PULLED ONTO STROUD GREEN ROAD LOOKING FOR SOMEWHERE TO PARK AND I FOUND MYSELF RIGHT OUTSIDE THE HOUSE WHERE I'D WRITTEN 'TRIBUTE', MY DEBUT ALBUM, MY BABY THAT CHANGED EVERYTHING FOR ME. IT WAS THEN THAT THE MOMENT HAPPENED. I SAT THERE IN MY MERCEDES, JEWELLERY ALL OVER ME, WITH MY GIRLFRIEND BY MY SIDE. I REALISED JUST HOW MUCH THINGS HAD CHANGED FOR ME SINCE I'D LIVED THERE AND HOW FAR I'D COME.

I HAD POURED MY HEART OUT IN THAT HOUSE. I'D SLAMMED DOORS, CRIED MY EYES OUT AND PUNCHED THE WALLS SO MUCH THAT I STILL HAVE THE SCARS ON MY KNUCKLES. NOW IT WAS PRETTY MUCH DERELICT, THE DOOR WAS BOARDED UP AND THERE WERE BIG BLACK STAINS RUNNING DOWN THE SIDE OF THE PREVIOUSLY SLICK, WHITE, ART DECO STYLE BUILDING. THE WHOLE HOUSE LOOKED LIKE A PLACE OF SADNESS. AS I SAT THERE, LETTING THE MEMORIES FLOOD BACK, IT FELT LIKE THE PAIN IN MY SOUL HAD DARKENED THE VERY BUILDING AS IF I'D LEFT A SHADOW BEHIND THAT STILL LINGERED IN THE HOUSE.

I ALSO FELT REMOVED FROM IT, LIKE THAT PART OF MY LIFE WAS DONE, FINISHED, WRAPPED UP AND CONTAINED IN THAT BROKEN HOME. I FELT LIKE I'D MOVED ON COMPLETELY, LIKE I'D LEFT A WHOLE WORLD AND PART OF MY LIFE BEHIND ME.

TO BE FAIR, I GUESS I HAD.

A house full of memories

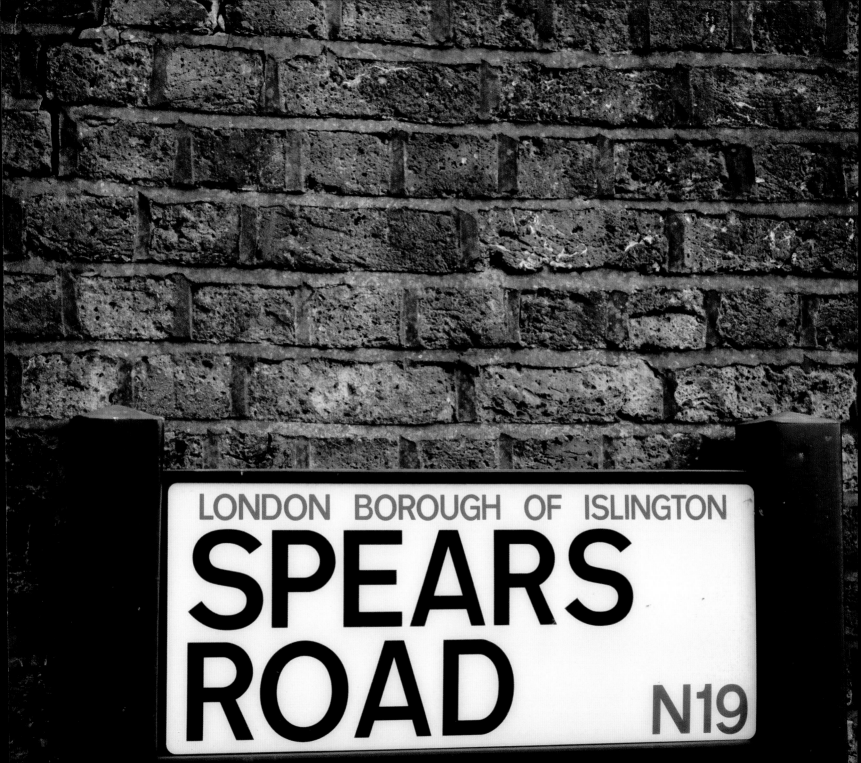

LONDON BOROUGH OF ISLINGTON
SPEARS ROAD
N19

WHERE IT ALL STARTED

Until I was four, my dad was at home, but he made it pretty clear he wasn't too fussed about us. I have blurry memories of when he lived with us but they're not the best. After he moved to a small town nearby to start a new life with a different family, it became just the three of us, my mum, my older brother James and I. Today, the three of us are still incredibly tight, my mum and my brother are still my best mates. My father, maybe not...

Although my immediate family was small, around one corner was my grandma and grandad. Around another corner we had aunty Joan and my uncle Dennis. Two miles further down the road my uncle Tony, my cousins Wayne and Ryan and aunty Julie. We were a pretty close network, we still are. It's important to me to try and make my family proud and take care of them if they need it. My mother brought me up with good morals, which I hope I constantly put into practice.

Until the age of fifteen I grew up in Stainforth, a stunning little village set in the North Yorkshire Dales. I had a pretty banging childhood. Bonfires, tree houses, BB guns, nicking wine gums from the local shop, building go-karts, BMXs and playing football with my mates. It was when I was fifteen that we moved to a council house in Settle, a nearby market town. It upset me; I wasn't completely done with my reckless country childhood. By this point my brother had moved two hours away, up to the toon, he went to study music at Newcastle University. It was once my brother had left and we had moved into a town that I went through a stage that I imagine a lot of kids go through at this age; acting like a little shit, smoking weed, fighting and getting pissed every Friday night. I guess I was just bored.

Even as a teenager, the small-town feeling really got to me, the thought of everyone knowing your business and if they didn't they would just make it up, so they could have a story to tell about town. It felt as though some people thought you'd fall off the end of the world if you ever left the place; the furthest people would go was Leeds to have a daytime mess up on a Saturday or Sunday or to watch the rugby on away matches.

James + me

me, James + mum

"EVEN THEN I WAS A COMPLETE PERFECT-IONIST."

Nowadays, I get abuse if I criticise Settle, or talk truthfully about how I found it growing up there. Of course, in many ways it is a beautiful place; go two minutes outside of the centre and you're in the most stunning countryside surrounded by breathtaking views. I loved being able to smash my motorbike around the Yorkshire Dales before I was sixteen, that was until I got caught tearing around the local rugby field opposite my house. A kind policeman put an end to that though, handing me six points when my driving licence became active and a stinking fine. As you can imagine, my mum made me sell the motorbike. Settle just wasn't what I wanted when I was a teenager. Let's say I was trying to work out my place in the world and ended up running into a bit of trouble in the process.

Maybe I was just a bit too different, but I definitely had my fair share of people starting on me. I became a paranoid wreck of a boy who never trusted anyone, I felt I only had to walk out of a room for a minute and people would start slagging me off. I remember there was this thing that went on for ages, where this lad decided to make up that I had stolen his phone when I was chilling in my mate's room (which I hadn't). He would look for me to try and kick my head in every weekend. Some of my friends then turned on me too; the people I had done a lot for and cared for would be the ones helping him find me.

I feel like everything happened for a reason. All the harassment made me mentally stronger and most importantly turned my focus from shit nights out to music.

Opposite:
John in Settle

21

A JOURNEY THROUGH MUSIC

That's only half the story.

When I was little, my grandad had this Casio keyboard (which I've still got sat at the back of my studio). It's one of those that plays demo beats and you can hit sounds like, 'DJ, 1,2,3,4' over the top of cheesy grooves. My brother and I would spend hours on it. Although we were just messing around, I was also getting familiar with the piano and how melodies worked.

Growing up, I was into RnB and hip-hop to begin with, then (thanks to my brother) I went through a stage of 'donking' hard house and old school garage. I had a period of DJing in my room; I had bought some cheap belt-drive Gemini turntables from a guy called Scott Horsfall who lived down the road. It was mainly funky house records I was mixing, which I used to spend hours searching for on Hard To Find Records. There were quite a few occasions when people would be really concerned about the amount of smoke pouring out of my bedroom window, because Scott Forshaw and I would be smashing the tunes and a smoke machine all night long. Although I continued mixing, I needed to earn a bit of money, so I started using my mum's compilation CDs to DJ with, to earn some petty cash from the likes of her mates' birthdays and weddings.

My mum loved Motown and Northern Soul; there was a huge scene for Northern Soul in the north of England that had sprung up whilst she was young. A generation of teenagers from industrial English cities going mad for the B-sides of Motown that were not hitting the charts in America, but instead were being shipped over the Atlantic Ocean. My uncle used to go to the famous Wigan Pier nightclub before it burnt down – a couple of decades later I was writing the very same name on blank CDs to give out to my mates, because Wigan Pier was now associated with banging hard house! Alongside all the house music I'd listen to, there was also everything from Motown, to punk, to hip-hop. From The Supremes to Led Zeppelin, David Bowie to Curtis Blow, The Meters to Limp Bizkit. I didn't realise it at the time, I was just listening to everything that sounded good, but I was building a broad foundation of musical knowledge.

It wasn't until I was fourteen that I started to become a 'musician', learning drums from my mate Ben in the back of the school music room, taking piano lessons and writing tunes on my guitar. I was still producing hip-hop and house tunes and mixing records. But I began to also listen to great singer-songwriters like Damien Rice, Ray LaMontagne and Ben Harper. They inspired me to begin writing slow, acoustic tunes. I was quite handy at DIY, so I decided to build myself a tiny little studio in the cupboard that housed the fuse box under the stairs in our council house. If I get into something, I have this undeniable drive to finish or achieve it. I am a perfectionist, whether it's building a go-kart or designing my website or album artwork. When I started building the studio, I'd sit there drawing my heart out in every lesson at school then hole myself up working away when I got home. Everything about music had grabbed my heart and soul. It was in this makeshift studio that I started blending my knowledge of production with the instruments I was teaching myself and learning at school.

You literally couldn't turn around in my DIY studio but my mum, who has always been so supportive, had given me that cupboard, the largest space she could find for me in our little council house, so I made it work. I had the crappest gear ever; an acoustic guitar, my grandad's keyboard and a battered, old computer that I'd had for ages, all hooked up to some really dodgy Hi-fi speakers. It didn't matter though, because it was in there that I started crafting my art. I taught myself the basic techniques, bringing together sounds from so many different areas of music. As long as I could express myself and I enjoyed what I was making, I was happy. I also started putting my voice over the beats, it sounded a bit sketchy, but I knew with work I could make it better....

Opposite:
John recording
in LA, 2014

Music, an urge to perform and a firm belief that the lessons would be full of fit birds, led me to choose drama classes at school. Of course, people took the piss out of me, but I didn't really care because the classes were building my confidence day by day. They helped me to turn around and say 'piss off!' to everyone who was trying to get rid of their own insecurities by ripping into me.

My drama teacher, Suzie Power, told me to take part in the talent evening that the school was putting on. Besides the thought of it feeling like 'death by nerves', I agreed to line myself up for the embarrassment. I'd been playing music in my drama class, a bit of piano and stuff, and I got a lot of support from the girls in that class*. These girls all helped with the self-belief I needed to perform in front of other people and they were the people that helped the numb feeling in my chest disappear. During this time, I discovered my 'last breath' technique – which is the last big breath I take every time I walk on stage.

In preparation for my first performance on stage at the talent evening, a girl called Rosie Hirst and I wrote a song together. I also did a cover of Mario's 'Let Me Love You', which was a big RnB hit at the time. I vividly remember sitting down and hearing the creak of the piano stool and the movement of my feet to the pedals, before I began playing the first chord. I couldn't tell you how I performed, whether I played anything right or not. I just kept thinking 'what have I just done?' and feeling so exposed, as though I'd just dropped my trousers in front of everyone. That was my first reaction to being on stage and performing in front of other people. Afterwards, I remember walking around the back of the science department for a fag with my mate Rob Farrel, he turned to me and said 'That was banging!'. I then walked back into the room which was packed full of parents and guests, not just school kids, some of whom were total strangers saying, 'Oh, that was actually pretty good!'. It was the first time I ever experienced anything like that. I still remember that moment every night before I walk out on stage and just before I take my last breath.

*(Thank you Becka, Jane, Georgia, Sophie and the rest, and of course you, Dave. Dave was the girl I had to give a pseudonym to, so her boyfriend didn't know I was chatting her up!).

After that, other things started falling into place. I began hanging out with a different group of lads from another village, Hellifield. Nathan Dakin, Jonny Dawson, James Craig and Tom Galloway – they were all sound and didn't take the piss out of me. They were the people who really understood me and who helped me step away from the cycle of being arrested every weekend for doing stupid things. I owe a lot to them, for getting me out of Settle and the self-destructive pattern I'd fallen into. Although, Hellifield was only a few miles away from Settle, it was far enough. It was in Hellifield that I recorded my first ever EP – in my mate Mick Cardus' garage; it was quite a step up from my cupboard! I also started doing gigs, playing at a local pub called The Talbot. Matthew Leadbeater, the owner at the time, bought me a little Tascam 6 channel mixing desk and a new guitar; it was a big deal for me and I really appreciated it. I couldn't thank him enough and I played in his pub every Friday night.

"IT WAS JUST THE REGULAR ROUTINE OF LIFE IN SETTLE."

Greetings from Settle

Opposite:
John against the
railings of Arla Food
This page:
Settle

31

During this period, my confidence began to grow. Before, I'd felt so low, whether it'd been from people ripping me and knocking me down, or losing my friends over some stupid argument or misunderstanding. Now, I had people supporting me, recording me, helping me and coming to watch my gigs. Sadly, my grandad had passed away, but in a funny way I felt he was also still helping me out. Before he died, he'd given me a projector screen. I would set a camera up and start doing my own photoshoots; I'd get my mum to come out late at night with me to press the button on the camera after I had set up various shots. I remember taking one against the railings of Arla Foods (where my mum worked), sitting on the floor. I had managed to master Photoshop and played around with doubling myself up. I started making my own posters and artwork. I got really into perfecting the look and feel of everything; as well as doing online promotional stuff. I was trying to build my own image, but most importantly, I was doing everything myself.

At sixteen, I decided I wanted to become a mechanic. I had been welding car parts together and cutting them apart with a grinder since I was twelve, and living in Stainforth. I'd spend night after night out the back, in the shed, attempting to build go-karts out of wheelbarrows and tractor starter motors. I decided I wanted to take it one step further, but in hindsight it was definitely the creative side of mechanics and panel beating I loved, rather than the technical side.

When it came to the end of school I was filling in my record of achievement; in the section 'What do you hope to be doing in ten years'. I remember writing, 'I want to own a car customising garage'. I decided to try and take the sensible route and also make the first step towards breaking out of Settle. I left school and went to Keighley College to study mechanics. But halfway through the first term I lost interest. If I did manage to show up, instead of spending my day driving around in my mate Leon's pimped out Saxo, I'd be at the back of the class asleep or writing songs on scraps of paper. I'd gone, totally.

Instead, I kept on going up north to Newcastle, to get smashed with my brother and to watch him do gigs with his band 'Waiting For Volkaertz'. They'd just signed to Kitchenware Records, an Indie label based in Newcastle. That really inspired me. I finally realised — and admitted to myself — that music wasn't just a hobby, I seriously wanted to make it my life. My brother helped me make the right decision with his own actions and his words of support. I decided to stop messing around and start doing things properly...

Opposite:
John's early sketches
Following pages:
John on stage in Settle

21 ►21A 22 ►22A

100

27 ►27A 28 ►28A

►23A

22

►22A

23

100

►29A

28

►28A

29

MOVING OUT OF THE SMALL TOWN

It was 9am on Monday morning and I waited in the reception of Leeds College of Music with my mum and brother. We all waited anxiously for my audition. There were two parts to the interview, the music theory test and the performance. For the performance, my brother had taught me a piece that he had played for his interview for Newcastle University, 'Wait In The Water', an old Gospel piece.

Finally it was my turn; I dragged my nervous body into the room, and everything just phased out. Eventually, a letter arrived in Settle confirming I had passed and had been offered a place on the ICPA course: The Introductory Certificate to Performing Arts or, as it was known by others, the 'I Can't Play Anything' course. It was the first time I saw this look in my mum's eyes, the look that has and will continue to drive me through my career – pride.

On the first day, we all gathered in the auditorium and waited for the head of the course to arrive. Eventually, the doors into the auditorium were pushed open; the aura of the man filled the room before he had even entered. He walked to the podium and took a deep breath and said, 'So, this is it ... you are now professionals, you are now musicians, music is now your life.' After these words, he left the room in silence; that man was called Dr Carl Vincent.

LEEDS COLLEGE OF MUSIC

Tel
Fax:
Email:

18 July 2008

Dear Student

Following the Board of Examiners meeting, I am pleased to i
have successfully completed your Music Foundation Program

This course consisted of two qualifications:

- Introductory Certificate in Performing Arts (Se
  December)
- First Diploma in Music (January – June)

You will find a breakdown of your unit grades and overall gr
qualifications enclosed with this letter.

Please note that if you have a conditional offer from Leeds (
the BTEC First Diploma grade that this applies to.

Your certificates will be posted to your home address in du
your address may change prior to the posting of your certifi
the Examinations Team on 0113 222 3413.

Completed assignments from 2007/2008 can be collected
(FE Programme Administrator) from 11 August 2008 to 22
between 10:00am – 1:00pm and thereafter once teaching (
Monday 22 September 2008. Any unclaimed work will be
December 2008.

If you have any queries regarding your results please telep
on 0113 222 3413 or e-mail exams@lcm.ac.uk.

May I take this opportunity to wish you all the best in the

Yours faithfully

Charlotte Orba
Assistant Head of Music (FE)

LEEDS COLLEGE OF MUSIC

Department Marking Scheme 20...

HOULT
...MPhil GRSM ARMCM
...A FRCM

...ry Patrons
...d and Countess
...wood

...s undertaken and a minimum of 108 p...
...undertaken and a minimum of 72 po...
...undertaken and a minimum of 36 po...

...score 6 for Pass, 12 for Merit, 18 f...

...om the total point score (see belo...

BTEC National Diploma
3 'A' level Equivalent

Grades
DDD
DDM
DMM
MMM
MMP
MPP
PPP

...plete a Major Project – this ...

...TEC National Certificate
2 'A' level Equivalent

Grades
DD
DM
MM
MP
PP

...EC National Award
...'A' level Equivalent

Grades
D
M
P

Telephone
Fax
Email

Friday 23 July 2010

Dear Student

I am pleased to inform you that you have successfully completed your Further Education course. A breakdown of your unit grades and overall grade is enclosed with this letter.

Your certificate will be posted to your home address in due course. If you think your address may change prior to the posting of your certificate or if you have any queries about your results please telephone Donna Fox in the Exams Team on 0113 222 3413 or e-mail exams@lcm.ac.uk.

May I take this opportunity to wish you all the best in the future.

Yours faithfully

Guy Scarlett
Head of Further Education

...FE Department Marking Scheme 2008...

BTEC Introductory Certificate

...The overall grade will be calculated from the best two... ...eloping Skills in the Performing Arts and depending... ...ces, either Unit 9 – Individual Showcase and depending... ...our Work. You will be... ...rded a Pass, Merit or Dist...

BTEC First Diploma

...apply to the 2008... you will cover 6 units on your... ...best only and points... ...as least 5 with a minimum ...ore 6 for Pass, 12 for Merit and 18 for ...stinction... ...stinctions across 6 units you would get 108 ...ou overall grade... be Distinction *. The table ...ely matches the final grade ...

		CSE grade equivalent
		C C C
		B B B
		A A A
		A* A* A* A*

Principal Philip Meaden
BMus, MMus, FRCO, FTCL,
Hon FTCL, ARAM

Honorary Patrons
The Earl and Countess
of Harewood

After a year, it was time to stop sofa surfing around Leeds and taking the train ride home every night/morning. I found a 16th floor studio apartment on Westgate Road, nice but small. Making the move was monumental.

I got myself a job as a glass collector at a bar called Milo; the bar's owners, Louis and Dave, were very music orientated and Milo, was immersed in the Leeds music scene. There would be gigs on most nights and it was the main hang out for Leeds' musos. My boss, Dave Knowlson, was constantly playing me his favourite music. The roots of which lay in deep America and he made the records my mum had played to me when I was younger much more relevant. The best part of working at Milo was that I began to come out of my shell, it felt like everyone in Leeds respected my ambition, which filled me with confidence and supported me. If getting drunk and dancing around on the bar every night, or performing in front of (sometimes) a two person crowd, wasn't going to sort my head out, what was?

All was good, yes, my cheap plimsolls from the market may have been ripped to shreds and my staple diet was Greggs' pasties, but I was settling into a city and taking in all it had to offer. However, suddenly, shit hit the fan in the worst possible way. A blow to my life that numbed me for a long time, it changed me for both good and bad, forever.

Just after New Year, 2009, I had a call from my mother. I was sat in my flat alone. As I answered the phone, I immediately registered the tone of my mother's voice. It was the same tone that had told me when I was younger that my grandad had passed away and I was now hearing it again. She told me that two of my best friends, Tom Rodgers and Ben Ineson, had both been in a car accident, it had been fatal and just like that, they were gone. Ben and Tom had taught me that I could break away from the small town we grew up in, that nothing was impossible. The news hit me so hard, it ripped away one of the most important parts of my life. I didn't take it well. I rolled around on the floor of my student accommodation bathroom, throwing up in the toilet and screaming 'Tom, Ben'. I would wake up and smoke joint after joint in my now trashed flat, the thought of studying or listening to someone try and teach me was the last thing on my mind. When I did try and go to lectures or tutorials, I would last ten minutes before breaking down and running out.

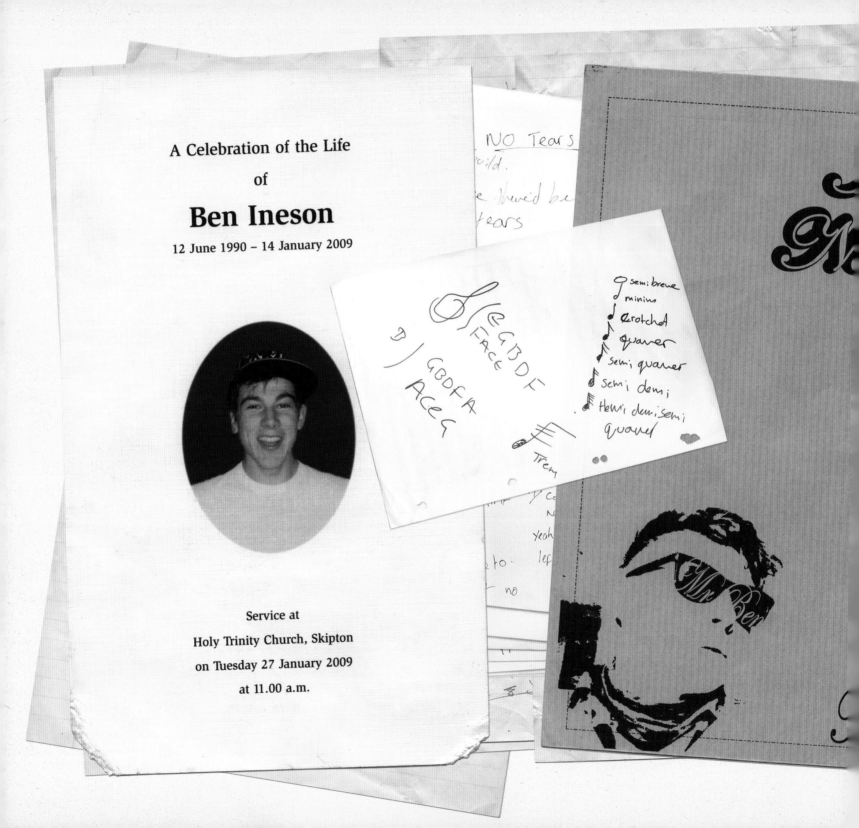

A Celebration of the Life

of

Ben Ineson

12 June 1990 – 14 January 2009

Service at

Holy Trinity Church, Skipton

on Tuesday 27 January 2009

at 11.00 a.m.

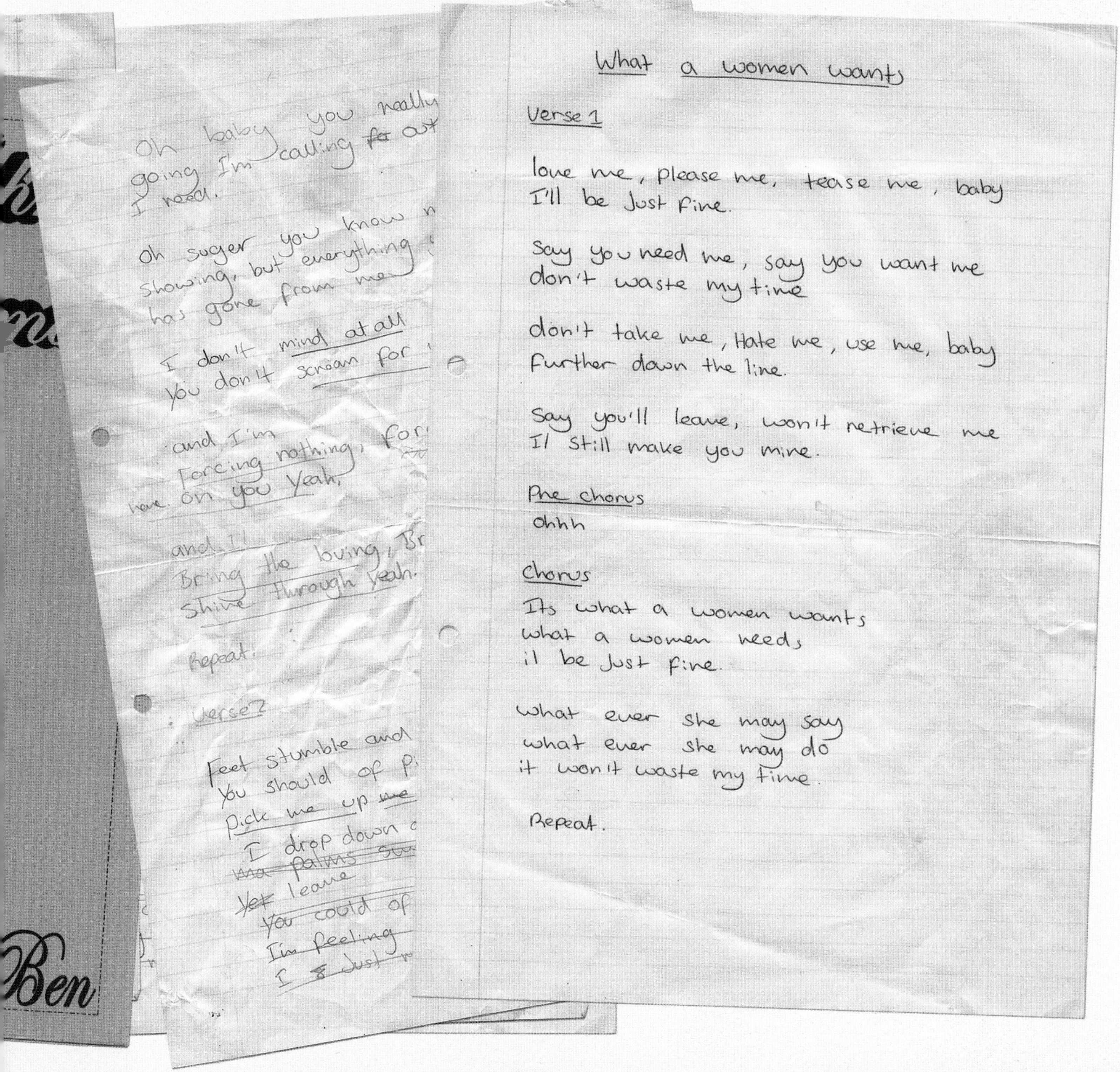

What a women wants

Verse 1

love me, please me, tease me, baby
I'll be Just fine.

Say you need me, say you want me
don't waste my time

don't take me, Hate me, use me, baby
further down the line.

Say you'll leave, won't retrieve me
I'l still make you mine.

Pre chorus
Ohhh

Chorus
Its what a women wants
What a women needs
il be Just fine.

What ever she may say
what ever she may do
it won't waste my time.

Repeat.

Oh baby you really
going I'm calling for out
I need.

Oh suger you know
showing, but everything
has gone from me

I don't mind at all
You don't scream for

and I'm
forcing nothing, for
have on you Yeah,

and I'l
Bring the loving, Br
Shive through Yeah.

Repeat.

Verse 2

Feet stumble and
You should of pi
Pick me up
I drop down
palms
leave
You could of
I'm feeling
I Just

Throughout the darkest days, there was one thing that was always there for me. One thing that could break the silence of my cold, dark apartment, it was there to pick me up off the floor, wake me up and push me through to the morning; it was Otis Redding's album 'Blue'. I had discovered it whilst searching for new music in the library and had borrowed it just before I received the news. I never knew then that it would be there for me throughout everything. Although, I ended up with a library fine of over £200 in late fees, I can't put a price on what that album did for me. To this day, it is still too hard to listen to 'A Change Is Gonna Come'.

Ultimately, that album changed me, I listened to hours and hours of the same songs and they penetrated my soul. The music sunk in deep. Although I was coming from a pop background, I started to make music that actually said something. At the time, I'd just written a song called 'Betsy' and the lyrics went something along the lines of, 'Day one, you came into my life, Day two, you said you miss me, Day three, you kissed me', basically, rubbish. After spending night after night rolling around on the floor screaming and crying in an utter state, I started waking up to find paper scattered across the floor with lyrics scribbled all over them. One morning, I picked up one of the crumpled balls of paper and read something that wasn't just emotionally charged nonsense; it worked and really said something, in the most simple, poignant manner. That piece of paper became a song called 'Mr. Ben', dedicated to my friend, Ben. I will never forget that morning when my songwriting became my release, my route in and out, for the best and worst parts of my life. I was performing one evening at the Cockpit, supporting a mate's band, my mother came to watch me (as she did with nearly every one of my gigs). It was then that I played 'Mr. Ben' for the first time. When I walked off stage she was tearful. She explained that it wasn't that she was sad or felt sorry for me, it was because I sang 'Mr Ben' with such pride, conveying all my pain I had been holding on to and Ben was standing there, right next to me.

"THIS IS IT, I CAN GET OUT OF THIS, ESCAPE THE PAIN THROUGH MY MUSIC. AND SO I PUT ALL MY TIME INTO THAT SONG, AS A ROUTE OUT OF THE DARKNESS."

It's all for you
It's all for you
For what you have shown me

It's all for you
It's all for you
For what you have made me

There's an addiction to telling people how you feel, to letting it all off your chest, and this drove me to work and gig every night from then on in. I started getting more gigs and began spending one or two nights of the week sober. I was picking up local magazines and would sometimes see myself in them. It felt as though I was starting to see the rewards from expressing myself, for turning my negative emotions into positive outcomes.

I had learnt a lot about myself and my music was now part of this mental process. I quickly began to learn that life is simply life, everything happens for a reason. Cause and effect; I had the piss taken out of me so I had moved away, my ex-girlfriend cheated on me which made me stronger, my father left us which gave me self-drive, and my friends died and I matured so I could handle any situation. I was learning how to turn everything into a positive, how to be driven and not to take no for an answer. When you find yourself at a roadblock, you must try and find a different route around.

Vocally He Is A Definite Competitor To Sco
& Ray LaMontagne - An Exciting Young Ta

John
Newma

Sunday 26th April

At The HiFi Club, 2 Central Road,

Admission Is Free. 12 Noon - 2.30am (Mid Session Band On

THE HIFI CLUB 2 CENTRAL ROAD LEEDS WEST YORKSHIRE LS1 6DE. TELEPHONE: 0113 2-

atthews

The MILO Observer

"CHEERS JOHN, YOU'VE BEEN A RIGHT LAUGH!"

Entry - £0   Entry - £0

6:00pm Sunday 12th September 2010

Featuring Live Music from;

The S.S.S.S.S
Chateau Berber
Germain

Followed by;
John Newman & Guests

(Will Newman, Mark Crossley,
Hayley Gaftarnick, Dave Knowlson,
Adam Richards and more special guests)

JOHNS FINAL LEEDS PERFORMANCE!

EIGER
Music Studios

Come down and say farewell
to John as he sets his sights for
London to pursue his music career,
Free Tickets available behind the bar

ecalndesign@gmail.com

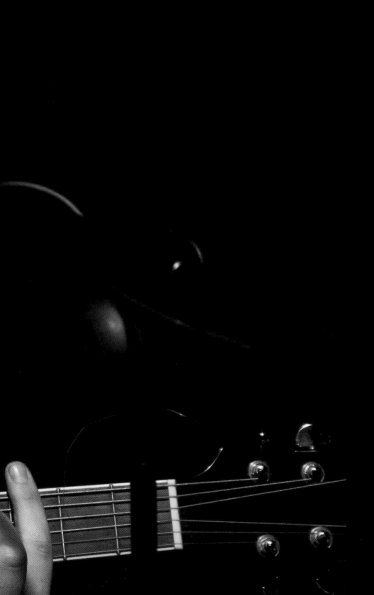

I learnt so much in Leeds and that was down to the people I hung around with, the good people, who reminded me to think 'I am a Yorkshire man, I am proud of who I am'. Although my mind was the most messed up it had ever been and I had found myself in some horrific states, I had sorted it out, I had worked through it and felt ready to continue my journey.

Leeds College of Music got me to Grade Six music theory and I was now pretty competent on piano, guitar and drums. At the same time, working at Milo taught me the other side of musicianship, about live performance, how social groups work and it built my confidence – even if I was just standing behind a bar, being an idiot, spilling drinks everywhere. When I finally left Milo, I got all the best musicians in town together and we did a big, collaborative set of live covers, it was an amazing night. The Leeds years were the time when the kettle properly started boiling, socially, professionally and as a musician. Leeds helped me to grow and turned me into the person I am today.

Opposite:
John on stage
at Milo, Leeds
Following pages:
Early press shots

51

THE M1 TO LONDON

One day, I was walking through the canteen at LCoM when I saw poster for a boyband audition. Everyone on my course was heading to the audition. I turned up at the audition and managed to use a bit of northern charm to skip the queue. I walked into the room to find a woman sitting in a single seat in the main auditorium; she had no clue who I was or what I was doing there (I hadn't applied and wasn't on her list). I told her that I didn't want to be in the boyband, but I wanted her to hear me sing. If the A&R teams weren't coming to find me and I couldn't get to the capital, then this was a good way to get things started. Jessica, from 19 Management, told me she would be in touch but for now she was going to carry on finding her boyband which, incidentally, later became The Wanted.

Jessica did get in touch and put me straight into sessions with an amazing songwriter, Steve Christian (aka Rae & Christian). Together we wrote two songs that had a very different feel to the slow acoustic numbers I had been writing. They were more uplifting and soulful, but still expressive. Suddenly it felt as though I was moving past the point I could ever reach in Leeds, it dawned on me that I had achieved as much as I could there. Yes, I was gigging every night and I was working with amazing people, but I wasn't progressing professionally, so I started applying for courses at universities around London. I remember my best friend, Tom, saying, 'are you really going to commit to another three years of studying, is that what you want?' No, it wasn't what I wanted, the student loan was what I wanted; a way to fund my career and move to London, until I got thrown out for not showing up (trust me, not the best business strategy). Thankfully, I was offered a place on a music production course at the University of West London.

I packed up my stuff in Tom's 106 and we set off to London. I was going to stay at my brother's flat for a few weeks, a warehouse conversion in Manor House. I was so pumped to get on with my career; I had everything ready in my notepads and all the tunes I had been working on ready to go. I wanted to make an entire album. I didn't want a record label or anything. I was just so fired up about what I wanted to do and I really believed in the songs I'd been writing. Once I was in London, I went down to Jessica's office for a meeting and started telling her about all my ideas, showing her album cover sketches, website designs and playing her the productions I had been working on. I could tell immediately my ambition was too big for her, she wasn't interested in my grand plans.

"I LIKE TO PAINT A BLACK WALL WHITE JUST TO SEE THE PROGRESSION."

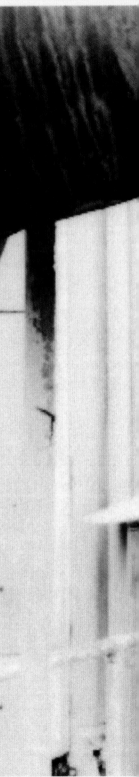

56 *Opposite:*
John aged twelve

"I'M NEVER GOING TO CHASE ANYTHING AGAIN. I'M JUST GOING TO WORK HARD AT WHAT I BELIEVE IN, NOT SEE WHAT OTHER PEOPLE CAN DO FOR ME."

I think Jessica thought she had some straightforward singer on her hands, someone who'd be thrilled to sing what she wanted. Instead, I was sitting in front of her wanting to write the songs, sing them, design the look and pretty much do everything. Eventually, she turned to me and said, 'To be honest, John, this isn't going to work.' Afterwards, I walked back along the River Thames for miles, from Battersea to Manor House. When I got home, I sat down at my desk in a smoky haze and just made music for months.

London wasn't easy at first; I'd been settled in Leeds and I had developed a bit of a name for myself as a singer up north. Here I was in London, starting all over again, going from being a big fish in a small pond to a small fish in a very big pond.

I wasn't scared, but it was hard getting my feet on the ground. However, things picked up when I got a job working in a pub, behind the bar at The Old Dairy in Stroud Green. I'd worked behind a bar before but this was very different to getting smashed and serving cocktails at Milo, it was one of those new so-called 'gastropubs' that had sprung up all over London, not very well suited to the working class. In the north, people just say what's on their mind, in the south they don't – they internalise it. As a kid, I always understood what people were thinking – because they always said it to me straight. Sometimes it made me feel shit, but at least I knew where I stood. In London people tended to not say exactly what they thought, they kept their thoughts to themselves; this new way of communicating took me a bit of getting used to.

60 *Opposite:*
Payslips and
Jobseeker's
allowance
This page:
The Old Dairy,
Crouch Hill

There were a few musicians that used to come into The Old Dairy. One day, one of my supervisors there, Sophie, told me I had to meet her brother, Piers Agget, he was in a band called Rudimental. I was introduced to this weird and wonderful genius; unaware of the huge impact he was to have on my life, both professionally and personally.

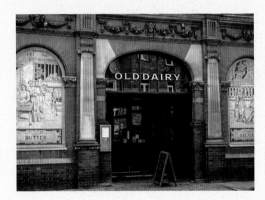

I hadn't been working at The Old Dairy long when I got the sack after giving a drink away; I was made an example of. Getting sacked put me in a really dire position; I couldn't afford to pay my rent. Piers and I had been hanging out a lot, and making a lot of music. So, when I needed to move out Piers really helped me, he invited me to come and live at his family's house in their spare room. The Agget family was so unbelievably incredible. Dot and Percy, Piers' mum and dad, were so lovely to me. His dad was an amazing musician himself, who had a serious music room, his mum was the loveliest northern bird I've ever met. Dot taught me how to be fifty per cent feminist whilst keeping the northerner in me. Percy taught me to care about the real music scene, not the industry around it. Piers taught me how to be me and his sisters were a pleasure to be around. I loved being in that house so much. Although I was on the dole whilst I was living there, I'd honestly be happy if I ever ended back there again. Thank you so much to all of you, I owe you everything.

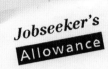

Jobseeker's
Allowance

01512
MR J W NEWMAN

Realpubs Ltd

COMPANY NAME:				Payment Method - Cash		Payment Period - Weekly	
Department 18	- The Old Dairy Bar/Floor Staff			DESCRIPTION	AMOUNT	DESCRIPTION	AMOUNT
					11.40	Total Gross Pay TD	2278.93
DESCRIPTION	**HOURS**	**RATE**	**AMOUNT**	PAYE Tax	24.54	Gross for Tax TD	2278.93
Basic pay	40.00	5.9300	237.20	National Insurance		Tax Paid TD	53.00
Holiday pay	18.00	5.9300	106.74			Earnings for NI TD	1904.00
						National Insurance TD	48.96
						Earnings for NI	343.00
						Gross for Tax	343.94
						Total Gross Pay	343.94
						Nat. Insurance No.	JK496633
				EMPLOYEE NAME			NET PAY
							308.00
DATE	DEPT.	PAY POINT	TAX CODE	EMPLOYEE NO.	Mr. John Newman		
	17		747L	1806			
14	11/07/2011						

STOCK CODE 0680 © 1996 Sage (UK) Limited. To re-order stationery ring 0800 33 66 33 (52804)

Phone...
TEXTPHONE for the deaf/hard of
hearing ONLY 0845 6088551

Date 25 August 2011

Dear Mr Newman

YOUR CLAIM FOR JOBSEEKER'S ALLOWANCE

You claimed Jobseeker's Allowance from 16 July 2011. This includes your backdated claim
from 16 July 2011 to 16 August 2011.

We have looked at your backdated claim and decided that you have satisfied the Labour
Market conditions for Jobseeker's Allowance from 16 July 2011 to 16 August 2011.

We have also decided that you have not shown good cause for the delay in making your claim
from 16 July 2011 to 16 August 2011.

This means we cannot backdate your Jobseeker's Allowance.

We will give you National Insurance contribution credits for the period 16 July 2011 to
16 August 2011 but we cannot pay you until
21 August 2011.

You claimed Jobseeker's Allowance from 5 April 2009 and 5 April 2010 to assess your claim.

We have used the tax years ending 5 April 2009 and 5 April 2010 to assess your claim.

From 21 August 2011 your Jobseeker's Allowance will be £53.45 a week.

If you are claiming for a partner

Your partner may be required to take part in a Work Focused Interview with a Personal
Advisor once you have been claiming benefit for more than 26 weeks. Your partner will be
notified if they are required to attend.

We cannot pay Jobseeker's Allowance for the first 3 days of your claim. Ask us if you want to
know more about this.

We may still credit you with Class 1 National Insurance contributions if you continue to
attend the Jobcentre.

Soon enough I managed to get another job and started working in a bar called The Silver Bullet in Finsbury Park, a spot where lots of musicians gathered. It was pretty similar to Milo in Leeds with loads of live gigs and DJs. It suited me a lot more, as I was back to working behind a bar, getting smashed, making music, meeting musicians, playing gigs and jamming. It was here I met Ollie Clueit, my soon-to-be manager. He was promoting gigs and ended up coming into the pub late one night. We sat down and got talking. He then came to a little gig in Chalk Farm and became interested in my music. He started to look out for me, putting my name about and making me aware of how the industry worked and the people I should meet.

I wanted to move away from the singer-songwriter acoustic sound that I had developed in Leeds. I began to bring in inspiration from the music I had grown up with. I was now living in a warehouse conversion in Manor House and one afternoon, a stumbling shadow appeared, out of a tent on the mezzanine. It was a guy called Jack Driver, an incredible guitarist, we would spend hours making tunes on his computer in my very small bedroom. Ollie also helped me pull together a band who I could work with (although I already had Piers on keys). I started to record some acoustic tracks with one of Ollie's mates called Johnny Harris, he is a bit of a musical scientist and could beat the hell out of the drums. Ollie also found Johnny Greenfield for bass. Piers' girlfriend at the time, Adiyam, was on backing vocals and his sister Beth joined her. That was the band. We started practising in grotty, little rehearsal rooms around North London, working on songs that I had been writing over the past year in my bedroom with Jack and through the late nights with the Francobollo boys at The Silver Bullet.

We were all pretty skint, so I bought clothes for our live shows from random charity shops. But I wanted to make sure we had a really unique style, so I would spend hours altering clothes on a sewing machine, with the help of my girlfriend at the time, Rebecca.

Ollie was getting us gigs every week, but it was my ambition to go further. Ollie and I were both learning the ropes so we decided that we should bring in an extra force and approached Paul McDonald. Paul, my now manager, came down to a rehearsal room on Camden Road to come and hear me play. All I can remember from that performance is that one of Johnny's drum sticks flew right past Paul's head, nearly hitting him!

63

Previous page:
John recording
in LA

I've never wanted to climb any industry ladders. I've always been the kind of person to enjoy the music that I'm making and fight for that kind of success. However, what I did understand about the music industry was that it was business like any other, so it was great to have people around me who knew how it worked, guiding me through the whole process. Ollie organised a four-track demo record, we recorded 'Cheating', 'Coming Back To Me', 'Stay The Night' and 'Nightshift'. We recorded at the Xfm studios with Chris Denman. I was still in a mess financially, so Paul forked out and paid for the band and also for Chris and I to have time in the studio.

Piers had always been part of a Drum & Bass group, called Rudimental (a group of mates who had grown up together in Hackney and Tottenham). One of them, Kesi Dryden, who I had started to get to know quite well, had given Piers an idea for a song. The tune had a really great hook and as soon as the guys heard it they knew it was something special, it just needed a vocal and some fine-tuning. I hadn't really done anything like that before, as I had never collaborated with anyone. I honestly didn't think it would be anything more than just going into the studio. It was a good song and I wanted to do a bit of writing and put a vocal on it.

I remember the feeling of walking out of the studio with Piers in Hackney, confident that we had written and recorded something really good. The song was called 'Feel The Love'. The Rudimental guys hadn't even really got off the ground yet, although they had already filmed a video for a song called 'Deep In The Valley'. Henry Village is the man who we owed the start of our success to, he helped launch Rudimental and was also the man behind Black Butter Records. He had such belief in us and started working his arse off, contacting record labels, trying everything, just to get the song out there; he believed in it. His charm worked. We secured a single deal through Ben, Matt and Ed at Asylum/ Atlantic Records, to release the track, billed as 'Rudimental ft. John Newman'.

"IT'S NOT A HIT UNTIL IT'S BEEN A HIT."

The second single, 'Not Giving In', was initially created when Piers and I were driving back to his house one day in his mum's old Renault. It had been pissing it down with rain. I had come up with an idea for a melody that sounded cool. So as soon as we got out of the car, Piers and I went into his bedroom and started developing it. I remember writing the lyrics down in my phone, the song was about our friend Max, who had just been released from a psychiatric hospital after trying to end his own life. I'd met Max through Piers and he quickly became one of my best mates. Piers and I both wanted to get him through this dark period. We never told Max the song was about him until just after I had performed it as it charted. The song is all about Max's inner demons and how he was going to overpower them, 'This time, I'm gonna be stronger, I'm not giving in'.

Between the time of writing 'Feel The Love' and when it was officially released, there was quite a long stretch – that's just the way the industry works – in the meantime, my managers continued to build hype around me and kept playing my demos to people. Thankfully, labels started picking up the phone, trying to find out who I was and what my voice was all about. There is nothing better for creating hype than 'timing' – exactly what you need to pull off a good Sunday dinner! I remember meeting up with Ollie one night in Islington and asking, 'When are we pressing the red button, when are we going to see the labels?' My managers were waiting for the perfect time to start pushing the Rudimental tracks, alongside the Black Butter team.

Because of the gigging I had already done, playing live was always very important to me; watching the legends like James Brown, Michael Jackson and Prince, who were all incredible live, made me want to aim for that level of perfection. I used to spend hours dancing and throwing my stands around Piers' dad's music room, just to make myself a better live performer. I didn't want anyone offering me a small, thin-paged contract and I knew the labels seeing me live would help. Ollie pulled together a couple of showcases in pubs around North London, including The Old Queens Head on Essex Road and The Bull and Gate in Kentish Town. Both gigs were rammed full of the 'right' people; heads of the music industry and everyone I had ever met in London. It was a good job I made sure the BVs were wearing different size heels so they were the same size, and the band wore the outfits I had slaved over for hours – they were a couple of big nights, looking back.

With Paul's insight and my own instincts, I knew the major labels could still be a bit old school. The problem was that they were the ones with the money, they were the ones whose deal I needed to be able to afford to live off. A lot of people get excited by record deals and rush into deals when, in the long run, they can't afford to live. I had been crafting myself as an artist; I didn't want to be sat on some dusty label shelf, before being dropped. I had been doing the rounds, taking up meeting offers from only the people I believed could really take care of me and who wanted to make me an artist, not a celebrity. I had pretty much decided on where I was going to go, until we had a call at the very last minute. I went in with my acoustic guitar and played a few songs to Darcus Beese and Ted Cockle from Island Records. Immediately it felt like a natural fit and they were clutching a contract there and then, wanting to get it wrapped up. So, on 12th December 2011, I signed to Island Records. I don't really remember that day as I got absolutely wasted; I still had to do a gig in Kentish Town at The Bull and Gate that night too, which I managed somehow. I remember walking on stage in front of all the people who had been supporting me, everyone was there, all my friends and family. I started my set with the words, 'Today, I signed to Island Records'. It was then that I saw the look again, my constant motivation, pride in my mother's eyes.

" THE DEAL HAD AN IMMEDIATE IMPACT ON MY LIFE. I WAS ABLE TO GET OFF THE DOLE. I REMEMBER JUST WALKING UP TO MY DOLE OFFICER AND SAYING, YOU KNOW WHAT? I DON'T NEED A JOB ANYMORE. "

Opposite:
John after his
homecoming gig
in Settle, outside
The Lion pub

The bank loan I had been searching for arrived. I paid Piers' dad the money I owed him and moved into a house with my girlfriend at the time. I'd been working hard for so long that I had built up debts to so many people and owed things to everyone, all in the belief that one day I would be able to pay back the money and fulfil the trust they had invested in me.

Signing to Island Records was definitely the most important day of my life. I remember thinking about all the people who had supported me; the people who'd worked so hard in my band; my mum, who has brought me up and always backed me; Piers' mum and dad; Dave Knowlson, my boss at Milo; Ben and Tom; Mick Cardus who recorded my first ever EP; and Suzy Power, my drama teacher.

All of these amazing people were in my heart and in my mind on that one, amazing day. As for all of the people that had ever talked down to me or upset me? I couldn't have cared less about them. I'd finally done what I wanted to do, what I needed to and it was all off my shoulders. I could now, finally, support myself, allowing me to make music my entire working life.

Opposite:
John on stage
in Settle

BED BOUND

At the beginning of 2012, my life was about to take another dark turn, one that I could never have anticipated.

Being a young northern lad, growing up consisted of regularly getting a kicking and falling off my motorbike. I was taught to get up, brush it off and walk it off. But this time I had a problem that had been really distracting me. I refused to go to an optician for so long, however, my eyes had got to the point where I no longer had a choice. I had bad tunnel vision and my peripheral vision had deteriorated completely. I had been hoping my eyes would just get better, that everything would be fine. Eventually, I went to get checked at the Boots opticians on Holloway Road. I knew it wasn't good news after the first round of tests – they immediately sent me to the eye hospital in Shoreditch. It was then that I realised something really wasn't right, I was also looking pretty ill and I had fainted a few times over the past few days. Soon, I was sitting in a hospital bed with a doctor putting anaesthetic in my eyes so they could touch my eyeballs. As well as numbing your eyes, it makes you go temporarily blind; as I waited for it to take effect, I went to look for my girlfriend only to find she had decided to nip to the shop. So there I was, sitting with my phone,

trying to call her – 'come on, come on' – but her phone wasn't working and every second the room became more and more blurry. Soon, I was incapable of using my phone. When they called my name to start examining me, I nervously made my way into the room, walking into almost every person and wall in the vicinity.

After the doctor had done all her checks, she told me I needed to see a neurosurgeon. My brother and manager Paul took me back to the hospital to see the neurologist. The specialist told us that she had 'a strong suspicion' I had a tumour on my pituitary gland (the gland that creates, regulates and controls most of your hormones, it sits at the bottom of your brain). That explained a lot: why my hormones were a bit out of sync, why I could feel emotionally messed up at times and why I always struggled to grow a beard! After that meeting, I sat in the pub having lunch with my brother, feeling like my whole world was falling down around me.

After numerous outpatient visits to the National Hospital of Neurology, my neurosurgeon confirmed that I had a 'mainly benign' tumour on my pituitary gland. However, I had left it too long, it was alarmingly large and they were concerned, they urgently needed to get me into surgery. It was from here on in that my mind started tearing itself apart; I was hiding it all inside and couldn't sleep at night. I feared being negative around others, I didn't want anyone worrying about me, but the truth was, I was a wreck and in a very dark place, everyday it was a struggle to operate. A key thought that I used to try and keep positive during this period was that 'there are people in far worse situations'; this knowledge helped me get through the run up to the operation. That being said, I would still not wish what I faced upon anyone.

Eventually, I received a letter from the hospital. They had booked me in for an operation, but they would have to call to let me know exactly when it would be, it could be anytime within a three-day window. When the call came I was walking to the shop; they wanted to get me straight into hospital, to begin preparation for my surgery the next day. My darkest day had come; my body began to shake, my mind generated everyway it could all go wrong.

The first night in hospital I rang my mum and girlfriend begging to come home and escape it all, I had never felt so alone. The next day, I individually met everyone that was going to be part of the procedure. It was time to head down to the operating theatre. My brother walked down to the anaesthetic room with me. That was when all my fears and emotions kicked in at once; I had never had an operation before and I was about to be tied to a bed so they could go through my nose to operate on my brain.

Following page: Early press shot of John

I was blinded I can now see

Opposite:
Early press shot
of John

When I woke up, I turned to the nurse and asked, 'Is it over, has everything gone okay?' I remember my sense of relief as I heard her say, 'Everything is fine, the surgery was very successful.' This was the first time, in a long time that I had been told that 'Everything was fine'. A huge weight had been lifted off my shoulders, I had got through it and a new chapter of my life was about to begin. I was wheeled back to the ward on my bed; I was still in a bit of a state for a couple of days, high as a kite and in agony. I'd had something the size of an egg removed from my head. After two days of tossing and turning and waking up at all hours, I was itching to leave. Everyday, as the doctors came onto the ward for their morning rounds, I would have already got myself showered, washed and dressed ready to go home. They made me stay for a week in hospital. It was a slow recovery.

It was an experience that I learnt a lot from, as it helped shape me as a person. Nothing seems that bad until it hits so close to home. I will never again take a day for granted. I will never take anyone around me for granted; if I love them I tell them, I want everyone to know how much I care for them. It is incredible how powerful positivity can be, I can now safely say 'my dark nights make my days brighter, the cold makes the warmth feel warmer', it's the bad days that make good days, 'good' days.

The first time I ever heard myself on national radio was whilst I was still in a hospital bed, not a bad tool for impressing the fit nurses I remember thinking. It was definitely an amazing mechanism to keep my mental strength up; although my health wasn't on point my career was continuing to grow, quicker than it had before. After coming out the other side, 'Feel The Love' debuted in the UK chart at No. 1. The initial taste of success was what I felt I had always been searching for, which then turned into a thirst. You have to be able to stop and take it in, be thankful and appreciate every success you experience in your life or career; otherwise you will lose sight of what it is you are working towards or for.

Craven Herald & Pic

THE VOICE OF THE DALES SINCE 1853

Thursday, June 7, 2012

INSIDE

SEVEN PAGES
of diamond
jubilee pictures
Start on page 28

**'I flew rhinos
in jumbo jet'**
Page 8

Singer, 21, celebrates becoming UK No 1

TOP OF THE POPS: Former Settle College pupil John Newman, who has topped the official UK singles chart this week

by Daryl Ames

Euphoria, by Swedish singer Loreen which won the Eurovision

Singer, 21, celebrates becoming UK No 1

THE VOICE OF THE DALES SI

TOP OF THE POPS: Former Settle College pupil John Newman, who has topped the official UK singles chart this week

by Daryl Ames
daryl.ames@cravenherald.co.uk

A young man from Settle is the toast of the town after he made it to number one in the UK Singles Chart on Sunday.

John Newman, a former pupil at Settle College, is the featured singer on Feel The Love, which is the first major release by East London electronic band Rudimental.

"I couldn't have asked for a better start to my career with the work I have done with the Rudimental guys," said John, 21. "We knew we were really on to something with Feel The Love, but as you can imagine no artist predicts they're going to make it all the way to the number one spot.

The song knocked last week's number one, We Are Young, by Fun, into second place, with

Euphoria, by Swedish singer Loreen which won the Eurovision song contest, in third place.

John started playing guitar and writing songs when he was 14 but moved to London when he was 20. While there he started a band, played a few gigs and was eventually signed by record label Island Records.

His band's keyboard player also happened to be one of the producers for Rudimental.

"When making the track we already had a good relationship with each other, which really helps when writing together," said John. "We will go on to do more work together and we have already worked on another single, unfortunately I will not be featuring vocally on this one.

"Regarding my own music there is much, much more to come. I

● **Turn to Page 4**

Previous pages:
Press clippings and
playing at Settle

This life ive been
living
This ~~the~~ love ive been
giving

This life ive been wanting
This life ive been needing
It's my life, it's my
tribute.

At 15 I had noone tobe
So confused, broken easily.

Now I could not be, half a man
without you here for me

18 you made me see
You lit lights id been
damperning.

You know I couldn't be
half a man, without
you next to me.

23 now ive taken in
The vicious world captured.
                  i was in.

My passion was abused
My words where never used.
But now i hope that you can
see.

Return Address
PO Box 200
Skelmersdale
Lancashire
WN8 6NY

08722SUKNW 10/2012

*Opposite and
this page:*
'Tribute' lyrics

87

MY TRIBUTE

Opposite:
'All I Need Is You'
original score
Following page:
'Tribute' ephemera

Telling your label, as a first time artist, that you want to direct the videos, create the storyline, design the artwork and then produce the album after you've finished writing the material gets them a little panicked. However, I really needed my label's trust, because when I began writing my album, I was going through a pretty bad break-up. I was in a bad place as my relationship with the girl, who'd been by my side whilst I was ill, came to an end. From past experience, I had learnt how to express myself in my music; it was time to release everything I had learnt over the years, all those thoughts and feelings into 'Tribute'.

The first track written for the album was 'Love Me Again'. It was written in a small studio in Parson's Green, with the man that I went on to do the rest of the album with, Steve Booker. Steve let me throw all my emotions and problems at him and did an incredible job of helping me channel it all into my music. The problem with 'Love Me Again' was that we all knew it was a hit from day one; I always say a hit is not a hit until it's been a hit – but sometimes you just feel it. The pressure soon hit home. I constantly found it hard to compete with the level of the first track. It summed up everything that I wanted to express about my previous relationship

and it pulled together all of my musical influences, it was a great debut single, but not a great song to write an album off the back of.

I have to thank Steve Booker for pulling the rest out of me and really getting into 'Tribute'; I wasn't short of creative ideas but he took the pressure off me when I still had an album to make after 'Love Me Again' came out. My first single was released at the start of summer 2013; it went to No. 1 in the charts and was nominated for a Brit Award for British Single of the Year and nominated for an Ivor Novello award too. My solo career had begun with an impact. Whilst I was promoting my debut single and my second single, 'Cheating', I was still pulling together my main project, 'Tribute', in the background. I called the album 'Tribute', very simply, to say thank you to everyone that had helped me along the way. 'Tribute' came out in October 2013 and entered the charts at No. 1. This first body of work had put me on a path, a path that kept me fighting for success.

THAT DAY, SITTING OUTSIDE THE WHITE HOUSE ON SPEARS ROAD, LOOKING AT THE BOARDED UP HOUSE, A CELL OF EMOTION THAT HAD BEEN LOCKED AWAY FOREVER, JUST ONE THING KEPT RUNNING THROUGH MY MIND.

'EVERYTHING HAPPENS FOR A REASON. NOTHING IS A COINCIDENCE, EVERYTHING THAT EVER HAPPENED TO ME HAS MADE WHO I AM NOW, I AM IN THE POSITION I HAVE ALWAYS WANTED TO BE IN, A PROFESSIONAL MUSICIAN AND, MOST IMPORTANTLY, EXPRESSING MYSELF IN THE WAY I WANT TO.'

I CAN NOW SEE THE FAULTS IN 'TRIBUTE'. IT WAS WHAT IT WAS AND GAVE ME WHAT I NEEDED, BUT NOW I NEED TO MOVE ON. I NOW KNOW THE MUSIC I WANT TO MAKE FOR MYSELF. THE MAIN REASON I AM WRITING THIS BOOK, IS BECAUSE I WANT PEOPLE TO KNOW THE PROCESS BEHIND MAKING MY SECOND ALBUM. I FIGHT EVERYDAY TO SHOW PEOPLE WHAT I SEE INSIDE MY HEAD, MY VISION, WHAT I WANT TO CREATE, BUT IT IS HARD. THIS BOOK IS TO TRY AND SHOW YOU IT.

JOHN NEWMAN

CHEATING

PART
TWO

I AM A PERSON THAT HAS A COMPLETE, 360° VISION OF WHO I WANT TO BE. IF I CAN'T DO THAT, I DON'T WANT THE JOB; I'M NOT JUST A SINGER, I AM PASSIONATE ABOUT EVERY ELEMENT OF MY BUSINESS, I WANT TO SECURE LONGEVITY THROUGH COMPLETE ATTENTION TO DETAIL. IT DOES GET ME STRESSED, I AM CONSTANTLY BATTLING TO TRY AND PRESENT MY IDEAS CLEARLY, PROVE TO PEOPLE WHAT I AM DOING. I LOVE IT, EVERY SECOND OF THE DAY I BREATHE IT. I GO TO BED WITH IMAGES OF LIVE SHOWS AND ARTWORK SWIMMING AROUND MY HEAD AND I WAKE UP WITH SONG IDEAS. I EVEN SPEND HOURS SKETCHING THE CLOTHES I WILL WEAR.

THE TRUTH ABOUT 'TRIBUTE'

Opposite page:
John walking off
stage
This page:
Song list from
'Tribute'

There are pros and cons when I look back at 'Tribute', I hear the flaws and I see the successes. I can see what I did right and what I did wrong. Even now, I still struggle to look at the cover of 'Tribute'. I had done all the sketching and had a clear vision, but bringing it to life was too much of a challenge. My label were against my ideas and there was the added pressure of time. My initial sketch for the album cover showed my friends and family in a washed out grey, stood behind an image of me in the foreground, the relatives and friends that had passed away were in the clouds above me. I was told by my label, 'this isn't going to work'.

When I listen to the recordings from 'Tribute', there is too much clutter; too many hooks fighting each other, muddy drum grooves and some slack bass. I won't let those problems slip back into my music now, it's just a case of learning from your mistakes. One of the things I love about the first album was that I made the music I had always wanted to make, as I always have and will continue to do. I never want to be involved in replicating what was No.1 last week, what is trending, or what is currently 'in' fashion. I want to stand out as my own person, in any given space.

Another important lesson I learnt from 'Tribute', which became crucial in the process of making 'Revolve', was that due to losing all my original demos (because of some silly disagreement), I lost that initial excitement you get when you first put an idea down. This was so damaging, as we then had to re-record each part of 'Tribute'. With the new album, I have been so protective about both my demos and productions; I wanted to keep the vibe from the early stages alive throughout the entire album. I have continued to use and reference the demos all the way through the process and have even added to them as we went on. For example, the first single 'Come And Get It' still has the very first demo vocal I laid down.

There are demo elements all over the album; vocal percussion, a lot of pencils hitting glass bottles and shoes slapping floors. All sounds that other producers may class as strictly demo content.

Opposite:
John on stage
in Settle at his
homecoming gig,
October 2013

The truth about 'Tribute' is that I felt like a young lad fighting for what I believed in, fighting to show people what was in my mind but with inexperienced, unconvincing and sometimes scattered words. However, now I know how to execute my ideas, I know how to tell anyone around me that is holding me back to 'back off'. I know now how to get what feels right for me.

It was new to me last time; bef signing and preparing my first albu was free to express myself in any v that I wanted to – this was the first t somebody had attempted to tell me wha do, it was the first time I had been critici I can take criticism now and I have hea all before, I have seen the trolls online the people belittling me. I experienced i as a kid. I have been shut down with creative ideas by somebody's unprom negative comments, just so it looks they're doing their job properly. But I ready now, its time for me to fight for w I believe in and enjoy the work that I do

MY FAMILY ON THE ROAD

Although I was concentrating and thinking about my second album, it wasn't my only priority: I had to keep promoting 'Tribute' and building my reputation as a performer and a good live act. I take great pride in my live shows. I will always pay meticulous attention to the smallest detail; what my band wear or the design of the stage.

There is one man who is my right arm when it comes to playing live, my show would be nothing without him, he is a man called Dean. I met Dean, when I was working at The Silver Bullet. I would often go in on my nights off, to get drunk for free and chill with my mates who all lived upstairs above the venue. One night I was there with my good friend Max, he got talking to a guy stood at the end of the bar – who I can only describe as a man who looked like he owned a whippet – wearing a flat cap, blazer and brogues. He told Max he was a tour manager and had looked after the likes of Amy Winehouse, Florence and the Machine, The Doves, Queens of the Stone Age and loads of other incredible acts. I thought the guy must be talking out of his arse. How could a man that has worked with all those people, be stood drinking in the joint that I worked in opposite Finsbury Park station? As we were speaking, he mentioned he had seen a video I had put

online; an acoustic video that my guitarist Jack and I had filmed of 'Cheating'. He told me that after what had happened to Amy Winehouse, he was done with the industry and wasn't interested in working in music again. That was until he had watched my video. It had touched him enough to want to work in music again, and he wanted to work with me.

So, 'that man from the bar' contacted my managers and continued trying to get through to me. Dean has now been my tour manager for two years. If I ever wanted a father, it would be him; he really is my best friend when I am so far away from home and when I need him. He takes my ideas and helps them blossom into a reality, in the quickest and easiest way possible. He really does embarrass the people that turn up to work and block other people's creative ideas, those that say 'no' to anything the least bit challenging. From the start, Dean began to help build the foundations for my live shows and when I say foundations, I mean my touring crew. They are the people who should be credited for the shows. They are the first up and the last to bed – the hardest workers in the business. I want to make sure I give my crew the credit they deserve and show them how much I appreciate having their talent on board. The first crewmember I began to work with, around three years ago, was Aaron (or Sharon), my in-ear monitor technician. He saw something in my shows at such an early stage and he put every ounce of energy he had into them. I also have Ryan as my drum technician, his long-term loyalty is incredible, he also has the balls to tell me to 'piss off', which I appreciate! My brother on tour is Drew, my guitar technician, he chats a lot of bull, but he's a complete pleasure to work with! The other man that has been with me since early doors is Mr John Gale, my soundman. Without Mr Gale, I have no idea what we would do with all the gin left over from the dressing room rider and we'd also sound pretty bad for the people that really matter at the show, the crowd.

Opposite:
John and his band
at British summer
time festival

I take great pride in my band because I have searched and worked hard to get my crew together, to create a family filled with such inspiring people. They push me everyday to work harder and perform better, because of the amount of talent they all have! I have Jackson on drums, my loveable little brother that always kicks my arse at table tennis, mainly because he is a genius at everything he touches. Jackson is the backbone of the band, driving us throughout every show. I know, I can be a handful to work with and one man that has to put up with me on a daily basis is Chris, my MD and bass player. He is one of those rare breeds of human that can execute my vision. On guitar is Carlos, he is from Mexico or somewhere like that, he claims to be more popular on the Mexican border than the guy who supplied 'The Wolf of Wall Street' but actually he just reads a lot of books. Carlos has had a massive involvement in the making of 'Revolve', I can't thank him enough for the love he has for his work. His wife, Cat, is also a beautiful person and an incredible photographer who worked with me a lot whilst I was in LA.

On backing vocals we have Rhianna. She is my very crude and wonderful mother on tour, who is always there to talk to when I need her. Alongside Rhianna is Adetoun,* she is the latest addition, we drove her slightly over the edge and she has now become just like the rest of us big pack of weirdos!

Admittedly, it's hard to go into every detail of each person's individual roles, as we truly are one family. We all go under one title. Everyone works so hard for my name, they are proud to be a part of it; we work together, as one. Thank you. I honestly mean that, thank you, I would be nothing without you all.

*When I did the first rough edit of this book, I wrote 'We recently got Adetoun in on the vocals too, she brings a certain element of calmness to the group – which I don't think she can hold together for too long'.

HIDDEN TREASURES

104 *Opposite:*
John on the stage
at Wireless festival

I felt like I needed to enjoy a year of madness to let it out my system. So I threw myself into every situation and just learnt from the mistakes I made along the way. Work hard and play harder. The summer of 2014 my touring family and I did just that, we saw the world and got the most out of every moment.

From falling out onto the stage of a medieval strip bar in Romania whilst my own tune was playing, to rolling around on the floor of hotel corridors with Tom, looking for the room's key card by throwing the contents of our wallets down the other corridor. Screaming the words 'Crawling Back To You' at Carlos most nights with a bottle of vodka in my hand, hosting hotel room parties at any opportunity. We saw it all that summer.

But, it all came to a head after a night out in London; I ended up at the Ace Hotel until the last possible second before my car arrived the following day to take me to a gig in Switzerland. I turned up at the gig and couldn't hit a note, I was so tired and I have never been so embarrassed and ashamed. That's when it had to stop, I had

experimented and had my fun, I guess I was rebelling against my punishing schedules. Ultimately, I will work non-stop, but sometimes I can't handle it and I have to smash that big red button and escape.

I learnt so much from every messy night we had. I feel like I matured, I know what to expect when there are talks of going out after a gig, I know the damage it can do to an artist's career. Get drunk one night and you're going to ruin both your performance and your voice the following day. I have to admit, I managed to deal with the hangovers like a trooper but I wouldn't do it again. I've learnt that I don't want to be a single lad about town any more, its not that great, you need someone to support you, to be proud of you and keep you humble.

After 38 festivals performances through the summer of 2014, we finally put 'Tribute' to bed. I remember walking off stage in Geneva knowing that was it, I had done all I could for that album; I had shut the door to that house in Stroud Green for the final time. The next stage was a dark tunnel, the next time I was to walk on stage was very far away and first I had to make a whole new album.

THE IDEA OF 'REVOLVE'

It was now time to iron out the creases and smooth out the rough elements of 'Tribute'. It was time to knuckle down and leave no stone unturned. I wanted this album to go global. That's a big sentence and to make it happen would take a series of actions to get me there.

Early on in my relationship with my manager Paul he advised me to 'turn the antenna on'. It was time, once again, to dredge through my 'bucket of influences' and start pooling together everything I wanted to add, in order to create stable foundations on which the second album would be built.

I have always wanted to be involved in the marketing strategies around my career. As I was looking for inspiration for the second record, I began to notice the distinctive similarities between the marketing of different high-end fashion medias. Magazine advertisements were always very slick, timeless and bold. I would spend time walking around high-end shops, being inspired by their designs and interiors. Bold logos; no offensive colours: black, white and gold interiors; art deco influence;

they all felt expensive and luxurious. Buying a product from one of those stores felt like an investment. I wanted to create a marketing strategy that was simple, a brand people would recognise and buy into. I wanted this for my album packaging. My ideas were beginning to form and were slowly becoming clearer.

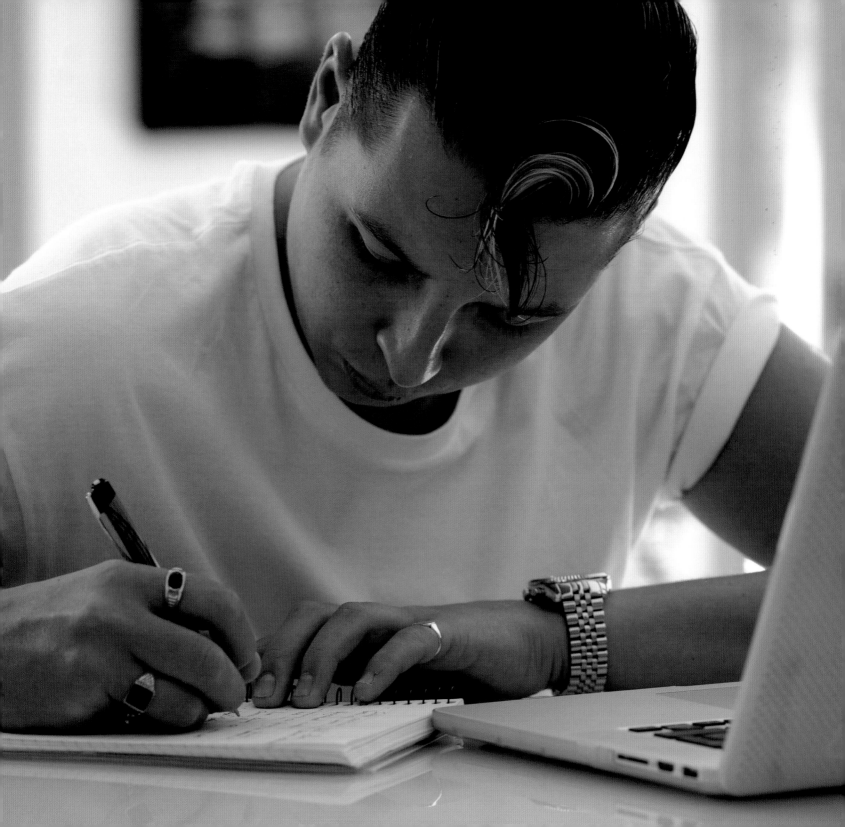

In December 2013, I saw my old best friend Tom after not seeing him for some time. I was back in Leeds, performing at the Sports Personality of the Year awards show at the Leeds Arena. He came to watch the show and we were chatting about his life. Tom was my best mate who had always inspired me with his commitment to life and his intelligence. He's a classical tuba player with two 1st class degrees and a lot of letters after his name, but he had become settled, his day-to-day life was repetitive, he was caught in a nine to five cycle. He would set off for work and return home at the same time everyday. He would sit down with his girlfriend for tea at the same time and then start the cycle again the next day. Friday and Saturday nights would be out with the lads, then on Monday it would be back to the same weekly routine. The same thing day in, day out. This is not necessarily a bad routine; it works for a lot people, there are plenty of people who love, breathe and live what they do, regardless of their working format. But Tom was not happy and had the thirst and drive to do more, to travel and explore the world. It led to me thinking about how different my life could have been if I had decided to stay in Settle, a life caught in a relentless cycle. A life revolving.

Opposite:
John in LA

This revolving idea began to merge with my ideas for album packaging. I decided I wanted to develop a circular logo, which could be used in so many formats. I realised that circles stood out from a page, from a wall, from a billboard, from a screen – all of which tend to be square or rectangular. I began taking note of the rotation of everything around me, the revolutions of the world; fashion; music; weather; seasons; time; relationships; life. Everything was revolving.

In January 2014, I was in the middle of an American tour and I had just arrived in LA for the first time; I got a buzz from being there. When I returned to perform at Coachella, I knew it was the place I wanted to make my next project. It had everything I needed to make a record that felt good whilst driving around in the sun. It was in Le Parc Suites Hotel, just off La Cienega Boulevard, where I really began to pull together my ideas. The concept of circular logos and the cycles of life became my central focus. I had a fresh new sketchbook packed full of ideas for my second album, which I had begun to call 'Revolve'. It was all slowly beginning to grow and become more and more real in my mind.

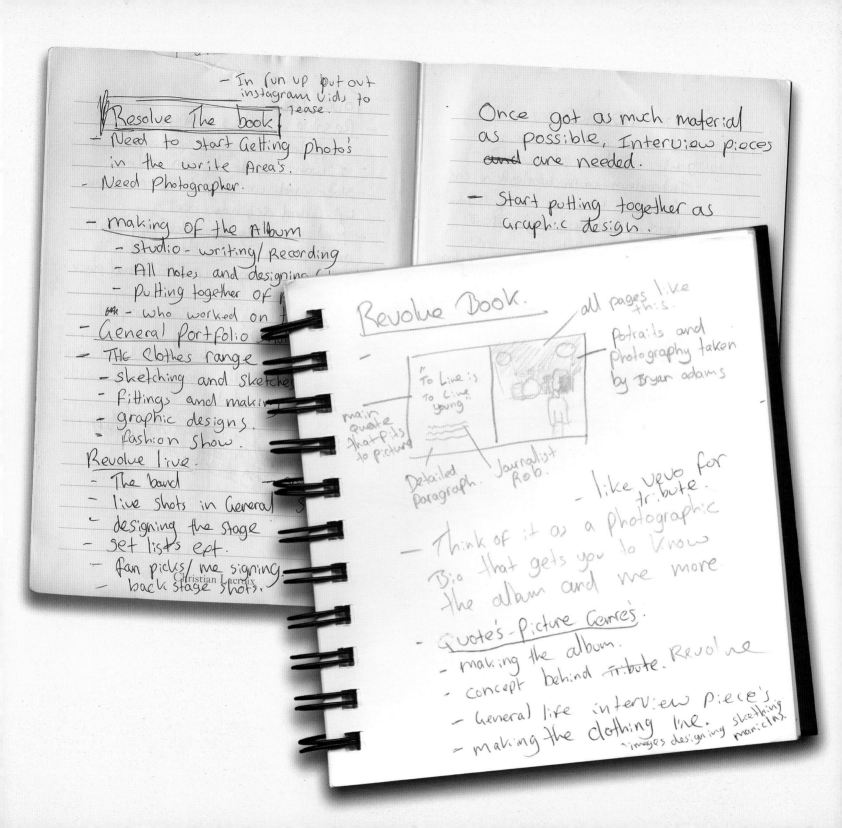

Left notebook page:

— In run up put out
instagram vids to
tease.

Resolve The book

- Need to start Getting photo's
  in the write Area's.
- Need Photographer.

- making of the Album
  - studio - writing / Recording
  - All notes and designing
  - putting together of
  - who worked on

- General Portfolio
- THe clothes range
  - sketching and sketches
  - fittings and making
  - graphic designs.
  - fashion show.

Revolve live.
  - The band
  - live shots in General
  - designing the stage
  - set lists ect.
  - fan picks / me signing.
  - back stage shots.

Christian Lacroix

Right top notebook page:

Once got as much material
as possible, Interview pieces
~~and~~ are needed.

- Start putting together as
  Graphic design.

Spiral notebook (foreground):

Revolve Book.

all pages like
this:

"To Live is
To Live
young"

Potraits and
Photography taken
by Bryan adams

main
Quote
thatfits
to picture

Detailed
Paragraph.   Journalist
                 Rob.

- like vevo for
  tribute.

- Think of it as a photographic
  Bio that gets you to Know
  the album and me more.

- Quote's - Picture Genre's.
  - making the album.
  - concept behind ~~Tribute~~. Revolve
  - General life interview piece's
  - making the clothing line. sketching
    ~images designing maniclns.

After two weeks of Coachella, we boarded a plane to begin my first mini-world tour. The first flight was to Dubai, which is apparently the longest flight you can take in the world they told us proudly when boarding (comforting!). After an eight hour stop-over in Dubai, where I had to buy women's clothing from a local shop because the airline held my suitcase, we then boarded our connecting flight. Another twelve hours and we finally landed in Cape Town, South Africa. I didn't really mind the long flights, I had so much to do and they were forcing me to get my head down. It gave me the time to get stuck into the second album concept.

From Cape Town we went on to Johannesburg, then to Australia for three days before finally flying back to London – my sense of time, my body and my mind were completely blown. For a kid from a small town in North Yorkshire, the whole thing blew me away, I couldn't believe my music had travelled that far: we had just sold out an arena in South Africa! The social intercourse and experience I was having as I travelled through such different cultures was way beyond any of my previously imagined expectations. It was this trip that opened up my mind to the world. Paul had told me to switch my inspirational antenna on so that I could fill my bucket of inspiration. During this trip everything seemed to fall into place, from the fairground merry-go-round outside my room in South Africa, to physically travelling a complete revolution of the world.

I'm screaming on your
drive way, baby screaming outside
your

I' need your love like before

safe me from this lonliness
pick me up off this floor,

►23A   22   ►22A   23

100   5 0 0

CREATING A REALITY

Throughout my work, whether I am designing the set for my live shows, designing my album covers, my website, book layouts or producing music, it all comes from my 'bucket of influence'. My bucket of influence is constantly being added to; musical influences, architecture, design or even just the colours I see everyday. The benefit of using this bucket technique, is that it creates a sense of continuity when progressing projects or ideas.

As I began to make my second album I was listening to a lot of disco and funk records, I compiled playlists that inspired me. I didn't want to rip off famous disco tracks, but I wanted to be inspired and influenced by them, to add to the bucket of influence I had created for 'Tribute'. Once I was ready and the ideas were beginning to spark, I went into the 'sketch pad period'! I sketched out circular logo ideas, concepts and started to put my ideas down on paper. Meanwhile, I was also beginning songwriting sessions and getting some demos locked down.

There is something beautiful about the sketching stage, you spend night after sleepless night, creating images and sounds in your head. Most importantly, at this stage you are creatively free – there are no budgets, nothing shoring you to the realities of the industry. When you want something so badly and you have a specific vision in mind, there is nothing more satisfying than making it real and bringing it fully to life, but this is also where the problems start. You have to be stubborn, committed to the vision you saw before you went to sleep that night. I have to fight continuously to show people what's inside my head.

23

29

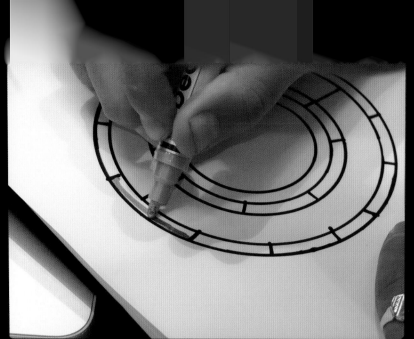

Producing the record you want can be very hard. You have to alter your state of mind, almost as though you are method acting the part you need to play. As an artist making an album, you have to over-exaggerate the emotions you have, your feelings that you have put into your lyrics now have to carry a song and hold a listener. You go through these manic stages; pieces of paper flying around your workspace with lyrical ideas scrawled all over them, track listings and sketches. The hard part is organising those pieces of paper, collating the ideas, pulling them into a format and eventually into a concrete final concept, bringing them completely into the forefront of not only your reality but those around you.

"I WAS SEEING CIRCLES EVERY-WHERE."

EVOLVING TO 'REVOLVE'

Opposite and following pages: John in LA

Even though I am very proud of the success of 'Tribute' and my previous work, I wanted more. I had work to do. In my mind I could always do more, if I worked an extra ten minutes a day, that's over an hour extra a week, that could be enough time to write a No. 1 single!

I wanted to provide for my family as much as I possibly could, it had become an addiction to me. The second I could afford to move my mum out of the council house we grew up in and into a new family home in Kent, I did. That's what keeps me hungry and motivated, my proud and caring family. Being able to look after them means more than anything.

I also wanted to start thinking about longevity. I wanted to stop messing around, so people couldn't use it against me and take my career away from me because of what the newspapers printed.

PART THREE

LIVING IN LA

LA is the most amazing place but it is a complete paradox. Some people have moved there and have been successful, while others have pilgrimaged and failed; LA can destroy your career or be the most inspirational leader. Housing the wealthiest and the poorest, the humblest and the most arrogant. The land of the free with an emphasis on authority.

I was ready to leave London. My relationship, which was well known in the public eye, had ended – people's opinions were starting to affect me. I found myself stuck in Shoreditch House most weekends, with everyone knowing my business; it felt like socially, I was right back to the small town feel of Settle. It was the perfect time to take a break, to go and spend six months writing, recording and producing my next record, away from it all, on the West Coast of America.

When I arrived, I needed to find somewhere to live; I often find the best way to discover a new place is to get involved in the nightlife. So, for the first two weeks in LA, Tom and I pretty much got utterly smashed every night. I learnt my first lesson quickly – every night you see the same faces in LA. The same people hanging off your arm telling you who they know and their relationship to various celebrities. You almost couldn't hang out with somebody new without questioning why they were trying to fill you full of shit like 'who they bumped into once by accident in the street', or 'which bottle bar clubs they hang out in and with who'. The funny thing is that none of these successful, famous people are anywhere to be seen! They're all elsewhere, probably working hard, not getting involved in the gossip scene.

There is a dark side that lurks, hidden deep in LA. When you are down, you feel the lowest you have ever felt, the bad days are the worse than they have been before. It may be the constant positive façade you are pumped full of everyday, so when you do wake up and 'smell the coffee' on the odd day, it hits you hard. Maybe it's because behind closed doors, all is not what it seems, there is sadness and poverty that plagues the city like any other. But the remedy to this? Take a step back, a deep breath and look around you, LA – the place is incredible!

After pulling ourselves together and beginning to appreciate where we were living, we really settled into LA's healthy lifestyle. California is a place of incredible natural beauty and productivity, if you use it in the right way, doing the job instead of standing about telling everyone how you do it! My friend, Adam, put me in touch with his personal trainer, I was eating dinner from Whole Foods every night, both Tom and I were training everyday, I felt great and it made working a whole lot easier. We were learning LA living, leasing different properties on a short-term basis, spending just over a month in each place and living all around West Hollywood, Beverly Hills and Bel Air.

To sum up the lifestyle and the social aspects of LA it is utterly amazing! But you just have to take the 'fame game' with a pinch of salt. I appreciate everything I have but I try not to take anything too seriously as I know I could lose it all tomorrow, so I'm just enjoying it while I can. If I get invited to an event I don't roll onto the red carpet with the biggest celebrity I can find – in fact I hate carpets, I get nervous and all my insecurities kick in.

This page: 127
The Hollywood
Hills

Opposite:

John's photo from
US road trip

Whilst we were in the States, Tom and I made sure we squeezed as much as we possibly could out of it; enjoying the nightlife, being productive and healthy and escaping it all and going out of the city.

We went on three mammoth road trips; the first was to the Grand Canyon. We took Route 66 out of LA and after thirteen hours of driving, stopping off in random museums and diners, we ended up in a place called Flagstaff in Arizona. There was just one problem, there was a huge beer festival being held there and all the hotels were fully booked. We ended up staying in a room that was close to derelict and the hotel was having major building work done, but it really didn't matter, we needed a beer and a bed for the night. After waking up at 4am and jumping back in each of the cars we had hired, we went to visit a meteor crater nearby. The most exciting part of visiting the huge hole in the ground was arriving at 6am, two hours before the visitor centre opened; the entrance was down a long, empty road with only a petrol station at the top, so we spent until 8am eating cheap hotdogs and racing each other up the road.

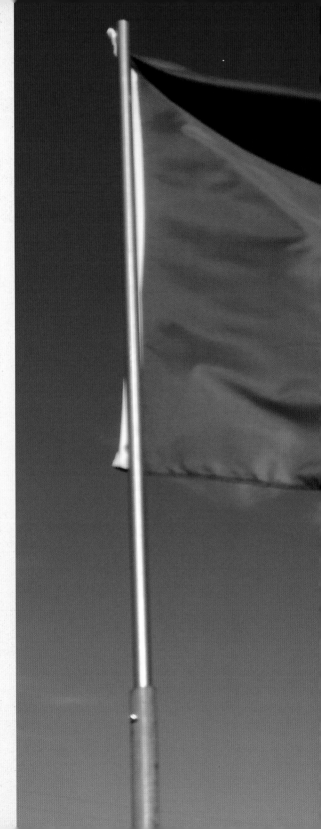

130 *Opposite:*
The road trip to the
Grand Canyon
Following pages:
John on Route 66

**GRAND CANYON
NATIONAL PARK**

01/18/2015   10:47 AM   601450
13   DAVID
16-709   #PER SINGLE VISIT   0.00
15-709   SEVEN DAY SINGLE VISIT   25.00
Credit Card   25.00
SUBTOTAL   25.00
TOTAL   25.00
TOTAL TENDERED   25.00
CHANGE   0.00

--- Card Information ---

Card Type: VISA   (Swiped)
Account #: XXXXXXXXXXXX0369

Charge Amount: $25.00
APPROVAL #: 086428
Date: 01/18/2015 10:47:20

Reference #: 117888131

Your Pass
EXPIRES
01/24/2015
NON TRANSFERABLE
NON REFUNDABLE

GRAND CANYON
NATIONAL PARK

SOUTH ENTRANCE
Valid at
Grand Canyon N.P.Only

Later that day we arrived at the Grand Canyon. It was there, standing over the vast chasm of naturally occurring space and beauty that it actually kicked in, what we where doing, where I had come from, and where I was now. I had fought to get my driving licence for so many years after that little police incident in Settle. I was now free to explore America with my best mate!

On other road trips we drove through Death Valley, down the Pacific Coast Highway, out to Vegas, up to San Francisco and, of course, called in at Disneyland! One of the most beautiful roads I have ever driven on was from San Diego, down into Palm Springs, the views are simply stunning. These mini adventures were our breathing space from it all; the showbiz scene, the fourteen hour studio sessions and the pressure of making a second album.

SONGWRITING IN LA

By the time it came to songwriting, I already had a very clear vision of the way I wanted my music to sound. I had been in writing sessions with an engineer, Bryan Wilson, and Carlos, my guitarist, in Miloco Studios back in London and on and off during my 'Tribute' tour. In the end I wrote five tracks by myself and eight with other writers. The hard thing was finding writers I worked well with; I know I can be a bit of a nightmare to work with, because I know exactly what I want and I want to get at it very quickly.

After getting together with Greg Kurstin earlier in the year, I came away with a track called 'Lights Down'; I really wanted to get back in the studio with him to write the rest of the album. Greg really let me speak and he really listened to me. He would study what I wanted from my sound and then we would experiment together until we found what I had envisioned for the record. I knew I wanted to mix in disco with modern house music, soul music with Tarantino guitars, hip-hop with Northern Soul, the modern with the old school. I didn't want to be tied to a definite genre, I just wanted to create my own unique sound.

As soon as I landed in LA, I got back into the studio with Greg Kurstin and the first track we wrote was 'Come and Get It'. Throughout the writing process I worked with Greg a lot, we wrote and produced four of the final tracks together. Greg has worked with Ellie Goulding, Katy Perry, Sia to name a few. What was great about our sessions was that it felt as though the real muso came out in him, I could see he was enjoying what we were doing, it was a pleasure to work with him.

Whilst I'm songwriting, I get the vibe and create rough demos first because I want to get all the hooks and melodies pinned down. Then, I turn the lyrics into part of my story. I know when I've found the right person to work with when they can pull what I want to say out of me. Steve Booker did just that on my first album. One man that helped craft my lyrical content on this album was a writer called Toby Gad. He is well known for a lot of his work, Beyonce's 'If I Was A Boy' and John Legend's 'All Of Me'. Toby is a pop pioneer with an ear for success.

During the middle of my stay in LA, I was having a dark day, which always seemed much darker when faced with LA's brilliant sunshine. That day, I had a writing session with a well-known producer, called Jack Splash (if you are bringing a new producer onboard, the best way is to often organise a writing session first to see how you get on). I poured my emotions into a track we worked on that day. All about the loneliness and the solitude I was feeling. That track became 'We All Get Lonely', a song that simply addresses the fact that we are human, and we all get lonely. Around the time I was writing with Jack, we had a gathering at our house on Scenario Lane. Jack eventually turned up around 3am, he decided that the best way to deal with how to get into the hot tub was to get completely naked and just use a towel, so when it came to driving home he still had dry boxers! A bizarre experience for the other hot tub users (namely only Tom and I). So, naturally, the next day I picked up the phone and told my label I would love to work with Jack!

MUSICIANS AND PRODUCING IN LA

I like to have fun whilst I am recording, so the listener can feel the excitement that goes into making a track. I smack the floor with the heel of my shoe, hit glasses with pens and generally just shout, scream and do vocal percussion. It's a great way of getting together my rhythmic ideas without going into too much depth before we record – I always end up leaving these elements in my recordings. I put all the rhythm, melody and general ideas for a track down myself first; drums, piano, bass and whatever else I can pick up and play. I'm a bit of a jack-of-all-trades, master of none though really...

I've learnt not to muddy tracks by getting too excited by each player, as this often creates a battle of sound. Everyone might like to have the best part of a record, but together in unison, we can create something far more powerful with much more impact.

I wanted slicker grooves with a tighter execution, so I brought in the best of the best to work with me. I wanted to create grooves that were addictive for the listener, music that would make people lose their minds! I had to get incredible musicians on board. After being so inspired by Daft Punk's recent work, The Gap Band, Michael Jackson and the whole general disco era, it led us to discovering a whole group of really incredibly talented musicians.

We managed to pull in Paul Jackson Jnr (Michael Jackson's guitarist), Freddie Washington (Steely Dan's bassist) and also Jerry Hey (Michael Jackson's trumpeter and brass arranger). Jerry wanted to work with me because he loved the demos he'd heard. Unfortunately Jerry wasn't very well, he was in hospital battling cancer, pulling together arrangements on a hospital bed. On the day we recorded the incredible brass section he'd pulled together, he was recovering from a bone marrow transplant. I will never forget what that man did for me and that very emotional day in the studio. It was the first time some of the players had been in the studio together since they had recorded for Michael Jackson; this along with thinking about Jerry made this the most touching session I have been a part of and it will always be in my heart.

We were based in Westlake Studios, Santa Monica Boulevard, Studio D, for the majority of our trip. The history in that room was both inspiring and overwhelming. Michael Jackson had the room purpose built to record his third solo album, 'Bad'. Earlier albums, 'Off The Wall' and 'Thriller' had been part recorded at Westlake too. I knew where I was working and I knew the musical history embedded within the walls, but I just had to be professional; I had an album to make and with the pressure of it being the second I had to channel this positively, not allow it to be another source of pressure. However, there was this one day in particular that it kicked in hard, we had to leave the studio. It wasn't so much the pressure, I just felt completely overwhelmed. The brass session had finished for the day, Tom asked Dan Higgins to stay behind and lay down some solo sax over the top of a track called 'The Past'. Dan must have put all the emotion from that day into that line; it was breathtaking, for everyone involved. When we had finished it hit me. I had just recorded Michael Jackson's saxophonist in the room that was built for him, the room that was overlooked by the special room built for his monkey Bubbles. I was in LA recording my second album with some of the best musicians in the world. Walking back through the reception and through the corridors, winding my way back through the building to Studio D, it was all there, the scribbled lyric paper of 'Billie Jean', the glove in the cabinet and the hats. It was incredible and awe-inspiring.

I want to thank every musician that played on my record; you are the colours to my black and white sketches. I would also like to thank Westlake Studios and everybody there, you guys provided me with a canvas. A special thank you to Matthew Brownlie and Jose Balaguer, two of the most talented engineers I have worked with, for staying in the studio until the early hours of the morning, giving my records your all.

Thank you, everybody.

Opposite:
John in Studio D, LA
Below:
Original 'Billie Jean' lyrics

WE'RE GOING TO MIAMI B**CH

142 *Opposite:*
John in Miami

I'd never been to Miami, but I knew it was a bit of a party destination, where people got smashed, it sounded perfect! We arrived on 13th February 2015, late in the evening. After making it out of the airport, being talked into upgrading my rental car to a psychotic SLS, we headed towards downtown Miami, where we were going to be living in a penthouse for the next two weeks.

Miami started out as stereotypically as the rumours had painted it (although it may have also just been what we were making of it!). We pulled into a high-security building complex, where I was told by Tom not to say the owner's name or apartment number – as we had to act like residents who had just lost their key! A sketchy looking woman came out and told us to quickly park the cars in the car park and she'd meet us in the flat. The worst part was the cars we had 'upgraded' to in the airport were not even a little bit inconspicuous.

When we finally got into the apartment, it was a stunning penthouse flat with a rooftop garden and three floors, far better than anything we could afford to stay in while we had been in LA. That night, Tom, my girlfriend and I went for dinner on South Beach, Ocean Drive, to check out how crazy Miami really was. (It was pretty mental.)

We were in Miami to work with Jack Splash and our first day in the studio together was at Hit Factory. We started recording the remaining ideas we had for 'We All Get Lonely', the track we had originally written in LA. Throughout the day, we had the choir come into record various parts for the album, Dwayne Bennett, choir leader, lay down some organ parts too. Jack is another musical scientist and a mental genius – we achieved something incredibly special together, both in his studio and at Hit Factory. Eventually, we ended up spending ten days with Jack in Miami.

Opposite:
John and Tom, LA
Opposite bottom:
John, LA
This page:
John and Tom, LA

From Gianni Versace's house to the streets filled with Art Deco artwork, I took so much away with me from Miami's ambience. The city is pretty inspirational; the views were outrageous and the people were great.

I loved my time in Miami and really loved working with Jack, I couldn't wait to get back in the studio with him, but I had left my heart in LA.

The one thing I knew when I left Miami was that I had captured 90 per cent of the album. The grooves were ridiculous, the sonics were slick and the songwriting levels we were achieving kept me feeling quietly confident.

HOME IS WHERE THE HEART IS

146 *Opposite:*
Recording in LA

The development chart Tom and I had created to keep track of the production progress we were making was so close to having all boxes ticked green, there were only two things left to do...

Firstly, we had to do the introduction. Secondly, we had to record the track 'I'm Not Your Man'. For this track I wanted to use my musical family, my band back in London, back in the studio I recorded 'Tribute', RAK Studios. This was purely for sentimental reasons. RAK Studios was the HQ of 'Tribute's' creation, it was instrumental in the creation of the rough British textures and dark undertones of that album.

'Revolve' was a huge learning curve, it took me back to where it all began, whilst also picking up and adding new influences and new touches during its creation. It slowly developed my sound whilst simultaneously raising the bar.

By returning to the UK to record 'I'm Not Your Man' I achieved a full cycle, the return summed up the whole concept behind 'Revolve'; I finished my journey in the place where it had all originally started.

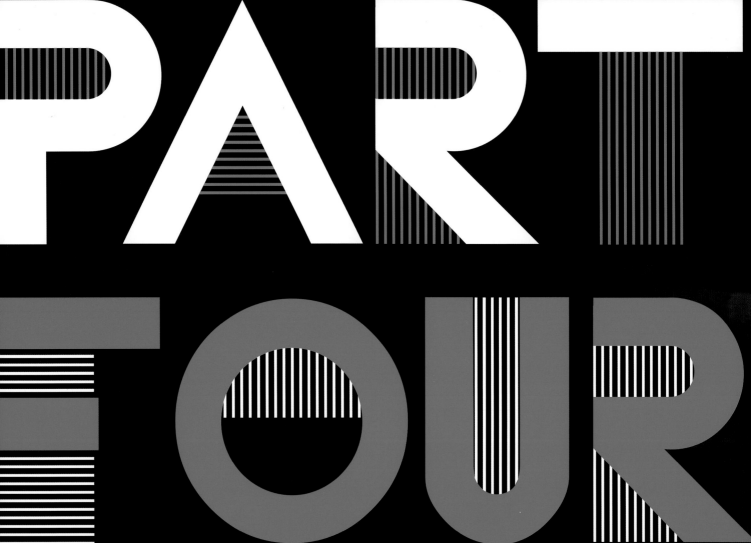

'REVOLVE' TRACKLIST

1. REVOLVE
2. ALL MY HEART
3. SOMETHING SPECIAL
4. LIGHTS DOWN
5. COME AND GET IT
6. NEVER GIVE IT UP

7. **TIRING GAME** FT. CHARLIE WILSON

8. **GIVE YOU MY LOVE**

9. **I'M NOT YOUR MAN**

10. **CALLED IT OFF**

11. **KILLING ME**

12. **THE PAST**

13. **WE ALL GET LONELY**

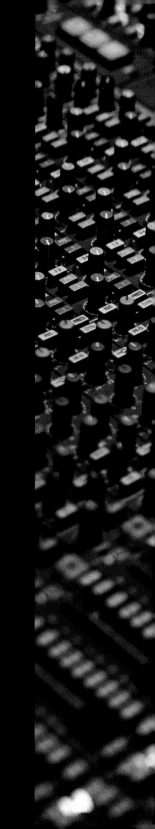

WE LIVE BY OUR EARTH'S CYCLES... VAST AND NOBLE.
FOR EVERY NIGHT, ANOTHER MORNING,
FOR EVERY STORM, CALM WILL COME.

WE LIVE OUR LIVES... BY PATTERN AND CYCLE.
FOR ALL YOUR LOSSES, A WIN,
FOR EVERY HEARTACHE, A NEW LOVE.

IT IS HUMAN NATURE TO REBUILD, TO REPLACE, TO TRY AGAIN.
WE ARE RESILIENT,
WE ARE STRONG.

IT IS COMFORTING TO REPEAT... FAMILIAR, YET NEW.
THE CLOTHES WE WEAR,
THE MUSIC WE LISTEN TO.
AND IN THE JOURNEY OF LIFE, WE WILL LIVE, LAUGH, LOVE AND CRY.
WITH NO CONTROL,
OR EXPLANATION WHY.
HAD TO ASK MYSELF, PERHAPS YOU DO TOO.

HAVE I BEEN HERE BEFORE
DO I CHOOSE ANYMORE
DO I REVOLVE
DO YOU REVOLVE

WE ALL REVOLVE.

We All Revolve

We live by our Earth's cycles — one and same.
For every night, another morning.
For every storm, calm will come.

We live our lives... by pattern and cycle.
For all your losses, a win.
For every heartache, a new love.

It is human nature to rebuild, to replace, to try again.
We are resilient.
We are strong.

It is comforting to repeat... familiar, yet new.
The clothes we wear.
The music we listen to.

And in the journey of life, we all Live, laugh, love and cry;
With no control,
Or explanation why.

I had to ask myself, perhaps you do too.
Have I been here before?
Do I choose anymore?

So walk that path again... or to chase a dream... in the hope of a win.

Do you revolve?

We all revolve.

1. REVOLVE

The main idea behind this book, was to express my musical vision to my listeners. I suggest listening to 'Revolve' whilst you read through this last section of the book. So you can see the craft and creation that goes into a finished album and how I executed it.

I wanted to reveal the concept behind 'Revolve' in the opening track of the album. I had the idea for the album fully formed, but the tricky part was turning it into a short and touching piece of spoken word. I put the brief out to scriptwriters but didn't find what I was looking for, they all made it too complex. It just needed to be explained simply.

A couple of months later, I walked back into the house on Scenario Lane in LA, after a long songwriting session and Tom, had a massive grin on his face. All day, he had been working on the script he thought I had pictured from the start. It was the most touching work I had ever read. It came directly from his heart – it was Tom who wrote and understood the central concept of the album. I just brought it to life, it was his life and he explained it in the end with his words. He captured not only how I lived in Settle but how he had settled down into the revolving cycle of everything the album was about; the world, relationships and life.

We All Revolve

Dear John~~

We live by our Earth's cycles… vast and noble.

For every night, another morning,

For every storm, calm will come.

We live our lives… by pattern and cycle.

For all your losses, a win,

For every heartache, a new love.

→ It is human nature to rebuild, to replace, to try again. *Love this verse ! x*

We are resilient,

We are strong.

It is comforting to repeat… familiar, yet new.

The clothes we wear,

The music we listen to.

And in the journey of life, we will Live, laugh, love and cry.

With no control,

Or explanation why.

I had to ask myself, perhaps you do too.

Have I been here before?

Do I choose anymore?

To walk that path again… or to chase a dream… in the hope of a win.

Do you revolve?

We all revolve.

For Idris Elba .

I began looking for somebody to record the voice-over for the introduction, which would give Tom's words the justice they deserved. I decided to get Idris Elba involved, we recorded him in RAK Studios whilst we were recording 'I'm Not Your Man'. Before we began recording, Idris turned to me and told me he could relate to all of the introduction, he had been there, he had grown up in a small social group and he totally understood what we were trying to say.

I'll never forget the look of pride on Tom's face whilst Idris read and recorded his words. We had both worked so hard to get out of Leeds and there we both stood finishing my second album in London with Idris speaking our words.

We got there, fella...

2. ALL MY HEART

158 *Opposite:*
LA studios
This page:
'All My Heart'
lyrics

When we were touring and promoting the first album we were constantly in and out of radio stations doing acoustic promo sets. It was while we were in a radio station in Ireland that I first came up with the hook for 'All My Heart'. I developed the idea with my keyboard player I was working with at the time, Chris Gulino, but it never felt quite right. However, I constantly returned to it and tried to redevelop it slowly over two years. It was while I was working in Miloco Studios with Bryan and Carlos that we pulled together all the new chords and verse material, it was Carlos that came up with the descending hook line you can hear on the guitar and strings.

The lyrics in this song are based on splitting up with an ex-girlfriend. She went through a period of not accepting or trusting my words or actions any more, shutting down anything and everything that I said. It was as though she wanted me to be honest and open and to say the words that she wanted to hear but had been fearing, to take the weight off her shoulders. We both kept fighting for the strength within our relationship. I eventually couldn't take my words being shut down any more – my honesty was never going to be enough.

"'All my heart, all my love,
won't give you enough,
can't give you enough'.

once it got to the point with ella where in her mind i didn't want her she had become so negative about her thoughts where, no matter what i did, no matter i said she still saw it as no good. it made me feel like is was no good for her, things had to change as i had become busy and we had to work around that however i don't think she could so it started driving us apart when we needed to be strong.

I produced this track and brought in Paul Jackson Jnr to fit over Carlos's original lines at the back end of the song along with the choir section I had recorded at The Hit Factory with Jack Splash. After listening back to the original demo, I decided to leave in the sounds of me playing the drums and piano and even all of my shoe slapping and vocal percussions (which you can hear throughout the verse). I wanted to leave a lot of demo elements in this track to keep its rawness. You can even hear the glass I was tapping on the first day of recording...

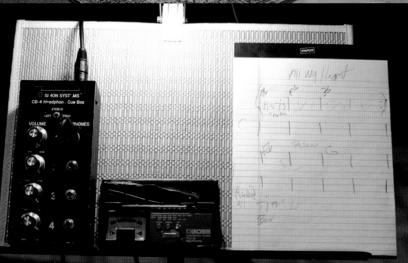
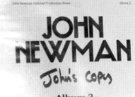

JOHN
NEWMAN

John's Copy

~~Album 2~~
Revolve

PRODUCTION NOTES,
PLAN & PROGRESS

3. SOMETHING SPECIAL

This was one of the first tracks I wrote for the album. I was on tour, and there were a couple of songs floating around, but they weren't really developing into anything concrete. I could see touring coming to an end and wanted to get some momentum behind me so went back to the studio.

This track has had quite the journey, it first originated from one of those sessions at Miloco Studios, whilst I was touring. It then came with me to LA and I began to lock a demo down. I had been working on 'Blame' with Calvin Harris around this time and you can hear his influences in this song. For instance, in the pre-chorus build I treated the hook line of the guitar with Effectrix (a plug-in that Calvin uses a lot). For the introduction, I used an ambient effect that I used in the first two Rudimental tracks too. I struggled with the second verse for a while, as it seemed too similar to the first verse. But this issue was ironed out when I worked on it in LA with the musicians who play on the track.

Although this was one of the first track ideas for 'Revolve', I produced it last. This helped me get some breathing space from 'Tribute' and remove the more 'Tribute' sounding elements to it.

There are still a couple of elements carried over from 'Tribute', which I quite like as it threads the journey between the two albums together, and that's why I put it early on in the track listing. In the middle eight – the bridge section – there's Morse code. I got the idea from the intro in 'Tribute', where we spell out 'This is my tribute to you' in Morse, which was my dedication to my mum. I used the same technique in the middle eight of 'Something Special', this time it spells out, 'We all revolve'.

4. LIGHTS DOWN

'Lights Down' was the first song I wrote with Greg Kurstin, on our initial day working together in LA. I'd taken in the sun and I'd started getting into the feeling of, 'What would I like to hear driving around this city?' so I went into the studio with Greg and made this absolute grooving beast of a song.

Greg and I played pretty much all the instrumentation except for the brass section. The complexity of the production work came in stacking the guitar line in the introduction and both of the choruses. We wanted to create a sound that was similar to a line by The Supremes or Frankie Valli so we stacked an acoustic twelve string guitar, an electric guitar with an octave pedal, a harpsichord and a little touch of piano. The string line that sits in the verse took a while to get right, it was about mixing the orchestral sound I often use in strings with the disco elements I wanted to bring in.

Whilst creating this song there was a real breakthrough moment. It happened when we came to create the groove of the main drop, we crafted a beat that sat right in between soul and house that I had been trying to nail for a while. A lot of dance producers and DJs side chain a lot of elements from the kick, and we used the same approach but with organic instruments; such as organ, strings, hi-hats and shakers.

'Lights Down' is a song about being on tour and living it up. I wrote the lyrics during a period of experimenting live and living on the road, enjoying it all whilst I could. I wanted to be single and I didn't want to get tied down. That's why there are a little bit more overtly sexual references in the hook, I wanted to add something a little hotter into this song than the other lyrics on 'Revolve'.

5. COME AND GET IT

ite:
nd Greg
n

'Come and Get It' was the first vocal I recorded for 'Revolve', before I even completed the song's lyrics.

'Come and Get It' is going to be the first single released off the album. I was always 100 per cent sure that 'Love Me Again' had to be the first single released from my first album because it stood out so much on 'Tribute'. Whereas, with 'Revolve' I feel confident that I've produced a lot of strong tracks, so it's been way harder to decide which track to go out with first. I deliberately wrote the album as single heavy because I wanted to create a really strong body of work. It's always pretty hard picking a single, as you become so immensely invested in developing every word and hook, but you need to take on board the advice of your manager and people who are more removed from your music. I always listen to my mother and my friend's thoughts, as they are the real listeners.

The comforting thing about releasing 'Come and Get It' as the debut single off the album is that it feels like it is a single drawn out from the whole of 'Revolve'. Whereas when I released 'Love Me Again' it was a stand-alone single followed by an album, as I produced the single then made an album.

Lyrically, it's about how I met my girlfriend. Usually relationships start positively but then can quickly become negative if it all goes wrong. Whereas in this relationship, it went from being a negative to a positive, I had to fight to get her. I first started seeing her in LA but she then had to go back to the UK, leaving me stranded and not knowing where I stood with her or us.

The vocals on the track are still from the first take I recorded after writing the lyrics that same day. The percussion is also taken from the demo. The whistling in the song was genuinely just me getting really excited about the track and we left it in the song. The whole body of the track came together within the first two days of working out the demo with Greg Kurstin.

23

►23A   22   ►22A   23

100   S U O

►29A   28   ►28A   29

6. NEVER GIVE IT UP

166 *Opposite:*
John in session

This is another song written with Greg Kurstin. We were inspired by the technique Michael Jackson would use, where he would get a riff and just sit on it.

It took us so long to get the verse melody right because every line was too similar to the lead line, but we managed to get the verse we were looking for in the end. The first verse originally had lyrics about a girl wanting to be the perfect domestic woman to me, but we decided to re-write the first verse and re-record the vocal at SARM Studios in London. During making this album, when it came to creating music, I strayed away from using synthesizers, instead I replaced them with organs or guitars but still playing a hook line that synthesizers would usually cover. Whilst Greg and I were making this track, he mentioned using a synth sound, it was the first time I was up for it in this project. I remember saying, 'If we are going to put one in we are going to do it with a lot of balls and a load of confidence'; you can hear this synthesizer solo through the middle eight in the finished track.

I want to love you,
but it just don't feel right,
I really need it,
but I can't stay the night,
because you never give it up ....!

7. TIRING GAME FT. CHARLIE WILSON

<u>In terms of collaborations, I didn't want to work with anyone that would put my name in the papers or be good for promotional material. But there was one person who has always truly inspired me and that was Charlie Wilson. Charlie was a part of The Gap Band and he has worked with Snoop Dog, Jay-Z, Kanye West, Pharrell Williams and Justin Timberlake. His voice is just ridiculous!</u>

I first met Charlie when I was performing at Jools Holland Hootenanny on New Year's Eve, 2013. I had the pleasure of sitting next to him during the show and that's how we decided to work together in LA.

'Tiring Game's' sentiment is a mixture between Charlie's own life and how my job was affecting my relationship at the time.

Charlie went through a stage in his life being a homeless drug addict. When he went into rehab he met his beautiful wife and together they pulled Charlie out of the hard times. Later when Charlie got cancer, they again battled it together. Being around this amazing human you would never be able to guess the struggles he has had to overcome, he is such a humble and dedicated genius. It was honestly a mind-blowing pleasure working with such a legend (and now good friend).

The other sentiment I was dealing with when writing 'Tiring Game's' lyrics was whether my girlfriend would want to be with me, as I have such a commitment towards my music and it has been an issue in the past. The lyrics in the second verse 'Slave to insomnia when I'm gone' stems from my girlfriend's bad sleeping patterns when she spent long periods of time without me.

Charlie's huge vocal at the start of the track was one take. What a vocal monster!

23

29

►23A 22 ►22A 23

100 5 U 0

►29A 28 ►28A 9

8. GIVE YOU MY LOVE

170 *Opposite:*
John in LA

'Give You My Love' was another track that started its life in London when I was working with Bryan and Carlos at the very start of the album. I then took it across the pond to the players in LA. By the time I began to work with Jack Splash in Miami, it was in pretty good shape. It just needed tightening up on the bottom end to give it a shine – something I didn't do in 'Tribute'.

I remember writing the lyrics very late on during my stint in Miami. My girlfriend had left to go and work in Europe for the weekend and I spent my time constantly calling her up, feeling very paranoid. I think my paranoia is a deep-rooted instinct from my childhood. When I was a kid I was treated badly in my first relationships and in early friendships and it still sticks. It mainly kicks in after long days in the studio when I'm exhausted and at night time when I'm lonely. When I am in a very dark place, it's important I express what's going on in my mind, to take the weight off my shoulders. When I am going through all these intense emotions writing is my outlet.

9. I'M NOT YOUR MAN

Opposite:
LA studios

<u>After a long day of writing with Toby Gad we had eventually come up with an idea (which always takes the pressure out of the beginning stages of working with someone new all day). Toby sat down at the piano and started to play this very Staxx/sixties/Motown ballad progression. After signing elements of what was later to become 'I'm Not Your Man' for around three minutes, Ollie Clueit, one of my managers at the time, came bursting through the door to tell me that it was the best thing he had ever heard me write – I told him he should listen to more of my music!</u>

Lyrically the song is about how I met my girlfriend. We met three years ago when I was performing with Rudimental in a club in Manchester. I was only a kid and struggled to speak to her as she was so stunning. We later met pissed up in London after I had been to the Ivor Novello awards and then decided to meet up in LA afterwards. I wrote this track when I was in the worst state of not knowing where I stood with her. It expresses all the frustration that had built up over time. Toby helped me get that into the lyrics, which helped me vent all my frustration into the track.

I finally recorded this following my trip to Miami; when I arrived back in London, I headed into RAK Studios to do a bit of tidying up. By this time, I had recorded the instrumentation for this track with my English band. I wanted to get the rough charm I had in my first album and there was no better place to go to than back to those RAK Studios. With the assistance of the engineer that worked on my first album with me, Robbie Nelson, I managed to get all that raw emotion I wanted into the song and the deep feelings that the track deserved.

10. CALLED IT OFF

'I'll be the sun that doesn't rise, shut the blinds and stop the light, so you can rest your tired eyes.'

My girlfriend suffers from sleeping problems and I wanted to write a song to show her that I would do anything however big or small to make her happy. It was also based on my time spent persuading her to be with me! I couldn't understand why we weren't together from the very start.

I always struggle to explain the meanings of my songs, because I want the lyrics to be what every listener makes of them, so they have universal appeal. Although being light pop songs in places the songs are really quite meaningful and come from deep places within me. I use music to say the things I can't let out in any other part of my life.

11. KILLING ME

'Tribute' was written whilst I was coming out of a relationship, whereas this album has more of a mid-relationship feel to it. When you make yourself vulnerable to someone, you open yourself up to danger.

The lyrics in the second verse express my deep fears: 'It's been six months since this began on a bedroom floor in la-la-land, times are changing, I've met your dad, I tell my mother you're the best I've had, You've got to stop this, You've got to stop this, Because your games are killing me.' I'm quite a paranoid character and when something's wrong in a girlfriend's life, I automatically think, 'She's playing games with me and she's cheating on me!' I guess this song was a way of expressing all that terror on paper.

Whilst creating the demo for this, Greg and I ran out of time and we had only laid down a very rough piano/kick-drum/vocal demo. In my mind I wanted it to be an easy listening track. Following a meeting I had at Universal, where I met the people putting together the 'Fifty Shades of Grey' soundtrack, I felt the tame nature of this song would be really suited to their opening scene. However, when this didn't happen, I became very single-minded about it, I decided I wanted to pull the full production together and head down the Arctic Monkeys stomp sound route. It just didn't work and actually slowed the song down. Instead we headed down the album route. It was the beat that was really key in the production of this track.

This track is a little different to how I would usually write. My lyrics are usually short, relatively catchy lines or long note anthem choruses, instead this track has a simpler pop chorus. This is the only track I have ever gone back to using programmed midi brass in parts, as I just couldn't get the punch back from using the brass we had recorded live.

12. THE PAST

178 *Opposite:*
John in studio

'The Past' was originally titled 'Love Gone', it's a mixture of two track ideas neither of which I wanted to lose. One of them was a track I had written with Johnny McDaid. We had the idea for a verse melody and chords but we could never quite get it to come together. I loved it though and couldn't let it go. The other track idea was a chorus I put together with John Hill. There was something about the chorus that wasn't quite working, it always felt a bit flat and didn't burst out like my other choruses tend to.

It was after I had returned from one of those drives across America with Tom, that I came up with a new chorus idea. I took to the new chorus because it gave the album a good breather from the ecstatic, high energy, high impact tunes I was pulling together at the time.

The song really developed when we went in the studio with Jerry Hey's brass section. Tom said, 'Why don't you just try Dan Higgins' – the great sax player – 'for a little solo over that song?' So we did. There were almost tears in the studio. We had all been grafting, grafting, grafting, until this point, where we stopped and said, 'We're getting there'.

I went out for a cigarette, just after we'd finished recording with Dan, and had a really lovely moment where I thought, 'This is very surreal, but I'm getting on with my second record. I'm actually doing it'.

13. WE ALL GET LONELY

Opposite:
John in session
with Jack Splash

23

After coming up with the idea for this track with Jack Splash in LA, it remained in its rough form for a long time. We hadn't pinned any structure down and it was a track that was continually forgotten (it was almost a surprise to my label when I played it to them at the end). This was the first track Jack and I focused on whilst I was at Hit Factory having landed in Miami, we decided to quickly sort out the structure and the middle eight.

When I was down in LA I was really down. It ate me up and made me feel very alone, especially as my family was so far away. When I turned up to this session with Jack at Westlake Studios I was having one of those lonely days. What brought me out of feeling so alone, was putting my loneliness into this song, it also helped me to come to terms with the fact that everyone gets lonely and it's part of being human. I wasn't actually alone, someone, somewhere else was lonely too.

I remember this being a huge ProTools file with around 40 tracks woven into it, we didn't want to take any of the demo parts out and instead added lots more on top. I remember whilst we were recording, the percussionist's chair was squeaking so we kept it in, I wanted ambient elements in there to give the feeling of loneliness. That's why, 3.07 minutes into the running time you can hear a door opening.

When I listen to this song, I can picture Jack sat behind the recording booth, with his big glasses on, grinning away and shaking his head from side to side. That's why there's loads of screams in there. You can also still hear me shouting 'Yeah' and clapping and smacking my feet against the floor.

▶23A   22   ▶22A   23

100

▶29A   28   ▶28A   9

AN ENDING AND A BEGINNING

There is nothing more nerve-racking than when an album is released. I've worked so hard to create this vision and make it a reality. I hope I have managed to express it in these pages. I know I have accomplished what I set out to achieve in this book.

As I write this I am sitting in the back of a car, just entering Birmingham, three months after recording the album. I am currently doing a promotional tour for the first single 'Come and Get It'.

To say nerves are gripping my life right now would be an understatement. I know if this doesn't work I have other options, I can try again. But I want to continue to make my mum proud and to be able to carry on giving her as much as I can.

I also have a heart fearful of failure, it's the perfectionist in me wanting my career to be the best it can be. Being successful allows me to design my own clothes, play my live shows, pay my incredible live team, make the videos I want to make, basically it gives me the freedom to do everything I love doing. None of this hits me whilst I am making a record or an album because I am focused on trying to make it better than what I have done before.

The fear only hits me now in the run up to release.

Wish me luck.

Thankyou

John X

'My first encounter with John Newman was on my daily afternoon break from a studio session to buy a Tesco's flapjack. I found him outside my studio complex with Mr Hudson, who he was making a record with. They were making fun of my car, as it had been shat on that day by an army of gulls. We've both come a long way since then; I had my car cleaned, and he has become one of the most exciting performers and songwriters of his generation.'

Calvin Harris

'Working with an orchestra can be stressful and intimidating for anyone. I was impressed with how clearly John articulated his ideas for strings. It's clear that he is a consummate artist, and the musicians immediately respected that. John was looking for something timeless. Anyone can add strings to a pop track, but creating something both lasting and classic requires deeper collaboration. John and I spent a lot of time finding the right balance between classic string elements and new ideas and textures.'

Joe Trapanese
The main string arranger on 'Revolve'

'I feel like meeting John, joining his band and living with him was the beginning of this wild rollercoaster. His passion to be an artist inspired me and I remember us having some of the best times together. Definitely a brother from another mother.'

Piers Agget
Rudimental

'After working with John in both LA and Miami, I learned that in addition to him being an amazing vocalist and songwriter, he is really one hell of a producer and that his ideas are endless. Both he and I have a lot of fun in the studio and like to go into our own little world, but that's only because we're both trying to make music that lasts forever. The fact that he plays so many instruments very competently made producing everything easy, because we knew where the tracks needed to go as soon as we started. The rest was just cooking up the strange brew.'

Jack Splash

'Regarding production, John is very involved in deciding which sounds should be present on his records. Our sonic tastes are very similar so it was effortless. What else struck me? John is definitely into cars. That's for sure! He's also a super nice guy and a very hard worker.'

Greg Kurstin

'I was already in love with John's hit 'Love Me Again' so I was really looking forward to our session. John struck me as a very intuitive artist who writes straight from the gut, with an incredibly strong voice. John doesn't overthink things and loves organic writing. I see some influence from Simply Red but I really haven't worked with another singer who reminds me of him. That's quite special.'

Toby Gad

'One of the things that all the songs shared in common was great production and great sounds. I didn't get the impression that John was looking for any particular styles from me. Rather, he wanted me to do anything and everything that would enhance the music. I like working with artists and producers like John because you're never pigeonholed into one particular style or sound.'

Paul Jackson Jnr

'When I first met John we were backstage at Jools Holland laughing about something, we became fast friends. When I watched him perform that night on Jools Holland I thought his voice and style were so unique like something I had never heard before. He was dancing and his feet were moving fast like James Brown. His performance struck me.

When it came to working with John in LA, John was very particular about what he wanted to do. I knew the mixture between his voice and mine would make an extraordinary record. When we sang the hook together on 'Tiring Game' and our voices fused it sounded amazing. The sound on the record is new and fresh. We had a lot of fun and making the record just came natural to us. What started out as two guys on a piano singing and grooving together turned into this incredible song. Recording with John was a pleasure.'

Charlie Wilson

PICTURE CREDITS

The publisher has made every effort to trace the photographers and copyright holders. We apologise in advance for any unintentional omission, and would be pleased to insert the appropriate acknowledgement in any subsequent edition.

Cover John Newman with thanks to MarkJames_Works

End papers: front Ollie Clueit; back Rachael Wright

5, 17, 30, 32-33, 36-37, 48-49, 57 61, 86-87, 89, 113, 128-129, 130, 155 John Newman; 6-7, 117, 131, 132-133, 145 Tom Willers; 10-11, 52-53, 81 Rhys Frampton; 13, 14-15, 60, 73, 96, 99, 101, 120-121, 124-125, 127, 147, 169, 171, 172-173, 175 Ollie Clueit; 20-21, 31 Vevo /Island; 22 Chris Allen; 23 Getty; 24, 27, 46-47, 56, 97, 103, 110-111, 152-153, 157, 179, 183 Cat Garcia; 34-35 76-77, 190 (below left) Kippa Matthews; 38-39 Alex Fergus; 42 Courtesy of Rhino Entertainment Company, A Warner Music Group Company; 44-45, 83 Julian Broad; 50-51 Suzy Harrison; 19, 68-69, 70-71, 75, Shane O'Neill; 84 Courtesy Craven Herald & Pioneer; 85 Shane O'Neill /Island; 90-91 Island; 63 Clockwise l-r Rachael Wright, Ollie Clueit, courtesy John Newman; 105 top Rachael Wright, below Ollie Clueit; 64-65, 93, 95, 108-109, 112, 115, 122-123, 135, 138-139, 144, 159, 166-167 Lucy Hamblin; 109-107, 136, 140, 141, 143, 148-149, 161, 163, 164-165, 177, 181, Rachael Wright

INDEX

ACKNOWLEDGEMENTS

I set out to write a book to make people aware of all of those who work around me. The people that help put colour into the mural of my life and work.

There are so many people I need to thank for my career (hopefully they are mentioned in the book). Firstly, I have to thank my family, my mother and my brother; James you led me to music and inspire me every day, mum your pride in me still continues to drive me every moment. Elizabeth, I am so sorry I didn't get you in this book, but you are the sister I never had. Thank you to my beautiful and continually supportive girlfriend – you don't ever let my work get the better of me.

Thank you to my manager Paul, for always picking up the phone and helping me develop my creative rants. Thank you to Ollie for assisting me in getting this book together, discovering me and giving everything you could to get me to where I am today. Tom, I thank you everyday and I will continue to, both personally and now professionally. Dean, thank you for making anything a possibility and for always supporting my decisions.

Thank you to everyone that has worked so hard to create this book; Romilly – thank you for working the long hours and the late nights. Thank you to everyone else at Quadrille Publishing, especially Katie Horwich. Thank you to Dave Brown who took my ideas from paper and helped to design a whole book and Mark James who transformed my 'Revolve' sketches into a logo. Thank you also to the man who I spent hours on the phone with and who documented my every word to help make this book, Rob Fitzpatrick. Also thanks to Clare Hulton, Emma Rowley and everyone else involved.

Thank you to all the people who were involved in creating my second album 'Revolve' and everyone that has been involved in my career. Thank you to my home label, Island Records and also to Republic Records. Thank you to everyone in LA that I have worked with, especially the photographers Cat Garcia, Rachel Wright and Lucy Hamblin, who have turned this book into the piece of art I had always wanted it to be.

I would also like thank anyone who is reading this...

Thank you.

Album Artwork.

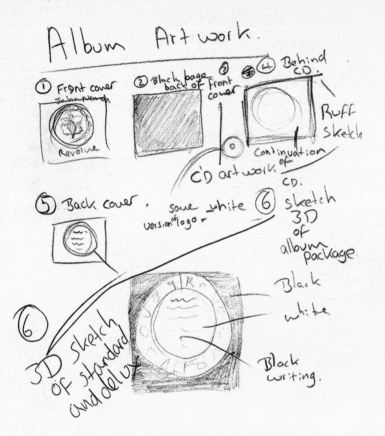

① Front cover
John Newman
Revolve.

② Black page
back of front
cover

③④ Behind
Front CD.
cover

Ruff
Sketch

Continuation of
CD artwork of CD.

⑤ Back cover.   same white
version of logo.

⑥ sketch
3D
of album
package

⑥ 3D sketch of standard and delux

Black
white
Black
writing.

② Back page of front cover

— Black Page

CD Artwork 2/1

JOHN NEWMAN
· REVOLVE ·
ISLAND

© all universal Island Records, a division
of universal music operations Limited.
® 2013 the manufacturing and
all rights of the work produced and the
owner of the

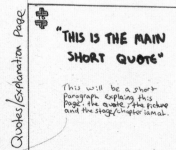

Quotes/Explanation Page

"THIS IS THE MAIN
SHORT QUOTE"

This will be a short
paragraph explaining this
page. the quote, the picture
and the stage/chapter i am at.

Photo PAGE.

Pictures
by
Bryan
Adams

FRONT PAGE

REVOLVE

BACK PAGE

Revolve - THE Book

- Revolve put into Quotes/pictures and Explanations.

EXPLANATION

A book that simplijfy's the understanding of how this album was made in everyway. From artwork, songwriting, producing to designing the live show. It will feature interviews of people working around me along with photo's of them and me aswell. It will show details such as sketches of designing the album artwork to just great potraits of me and others to capture whatever is needed. I want it to grip the reader visually with photo's on the right side of the page (apart from chapter pages). I want Bryan Adams to take these photo's, like Bryan Adams captures John Newman or Revolve. On the left side of the page i want at the top in bold black writing a quote that captures everything on the page, below a paragraph going into more detail. Imagine this to be like what revolift was for TRIBUTE

CHAPTER EXAMPLE'S ↓ Including:

- Concept of Revolue - The Revolue concept speech - Building the ADvert.

- writing the album
- Producing the album   - creating the live show.
- ARtwork   ext ext

FRONT COVER

CD ARTWORK

BACK COVER